Wake Up Laughing

Also by Pat Schneider

LIBRETTI
The Lament of Michal
Autumn Setting
I Have a Dream
My Holy Mountain

PLAYS
The Undertaking
After the Applebox
A Question of Place
Berries Red
Dream: The Musical

POETRY
White River Junction
Long Way Home
Olive Street Transfer

NONFICTION
In Our Own Voices: Writings by Women
in Low-Income Housing

The Writer as an Artist: A New Approach
to Writing Alone and With Others

Wake Up Laughing

A SPIRITUAL
AUTOBIOGRAPHY

PAT SCHNEIDER

NEGATIVE
CAPABILITY
PRESS

Copyright © 1997 by Pat Schneider
Turtle icon by Evan David © 1995 by Far Fetched Imports, Inc.

All rights reserved. No part of this work may be reproduced or transmitted in any form or by any means, electronic or mechanical, including photocopying and recording, or by any information storage or retrieval system, except as may be expressly permitted by the 1976 Copyright Act or in writing by the publisher, except brief quotations for the purposes of review.

Some poems in this book have appeared in the following publications, to whose editors grateful acknowledgment is made for permission to reprint: "Cyclone" in *Ms. Magazine;* "Máire, Who Feeds the Wild Cat" in *If I had My Life to Live Over I Would Pick More Daisies;* "Sound of the Night Train" in *Negative Capability;* "Personal Address" and "Letting Go," in *Long Way Home;* "Mama" in *Excursus;* "Olive Street Transfer" in *Room of One's Own* and "Nellie Gray" in *CQ.*

Photographs of Leona Davis; Sam Vought; Máire O'Donohue; Mt. Zion;
St. Louis and Ireland sites by Pat Schneider
Photograph of Pat Schneider at old Quaker Cemetery by Máire O'Donohue

Schneider, Pat, 1934–
Wake up laughing: a spiritual autobiography/ Pat Schneider.
ISBN 0-942544-54-4 (hard) 0-94544-53-6 (paperback)
Library of Congress Catalog Card Number: 96-069291

Book design by Barbara Werden

Requests for such permissions should be addressed to:

Negative Capability Press
62 Ridgelawn Drive East
Mobile, Alabama 36608
(334) 343-6163
Publisher: Sue Walker

For all my people

most especially
Rebecca, Laurel, Paul and Bethany

ACKNOWLEDGMENTS

A BOOK like this could contain a list of acknowledgments as long as the book itself, including all one's relatives: the fossil in the rock; the rock itself; the crawdad; the grandmother.

To all of those who have heard pieces of my story and have affirmed the telling, I offer my deepest gratitude. I thank my writing companions — members of my writing workshops in this country and abroad — among whom most of these pieces first came to articulation.

For a close critical reading of the entire manuscript and careful, line-by-line responses I am enormously grateful to Barbara Bosma Van Noord, Margot Hennessey, Anna Kirwan, Janet Longe Sadler, Elise Turner, my daughters Rebecca, Laurel, and Bethany, and my son, Paul. For making this actual book exist in time and space, for their encouragement and belief, I thank my husband and partner, Peter; my publisher, Sue Walker; my book designer, Barbara Werden; and my agent, Emilie Jacobson.

I am grateful to shadowy ancestors, and to my mother, Lelah Ridgway Vought, and my father, Cleve S. Vogt, through whom the ancient grandmothers and grandfathers have passed to me their dreaming. Love and thanks to Betty Shuppert for talking me into calling my father one afternoon when I was visiting her in Missouri, and to Mary Mackley for giving me the magical little image of the turtle and the spiral.

Above all, for permission to tell his story as well as my own, my heart's deepest thanks to my brother, Sam. And for their blessings when it mattered most, I bow to Jungian teacher Edith Sullwold, Irish nun Máire O'Donohoe and Lakota Elderwoman Eunice Larrabee, all of whom welcomed me home.

> . . . there is an angle of experience where the dark is distilled into light: either here or hereafter, in or out of time: where our tragic fate finds itself with perfect pitch, and goes straight to the key which creation was composed in. . . . groaning as we may be, we move in the figure of a dance, and so moving, we trace the outline of the mystery.
>
> CHRISTOPHER FRY

> I urge each one of us here to reach down into that deep place of knowledge inside herself and touch that terror and loathing of any difference that lives there. See whose face it wears.
>
> AUDRE LORDE

> The longer I am a writer — so long now that my writing finger is periodically numb — the better I understand what writing is; what its function is; what it is supposed to do. I learn that the writer's pen is a microphone held up to the mouths of ancestors and even stones of long ago.
>
> ALICE WALKER

Wake Up Laughing

1

WHEN I was thirteen years old, a knock came on my door. My door would open, if I opened it, onto a dark hallway in a tenement house in St. Louis. Behind me would be two small rooms.

The year was 1947; I had been told never, never to open the door when Mama was not at home. But the voice calling to me outside the door was familiar. As if a bolt of lightning had struck my heart, I recognized the voice: my school teacher, Miss Dunn, whom I adored.

It was unthinkable that a seventh grade teacher would visit one of her students. It was unbearable that Miss Dunn had come up the dirty stairs, that she had climbed three flights, that she might see the clutter, the dirt, the shame in the rooms behind me.

The school year was over. It was summer, hot and sticky in that Mississippi river-bottom air. I opened the door just the tiniest crack, with the chain lock still in place. Yes. It was true. Miss Dunn stood in the dim light of the hallway, and she was smiling at me.

I unlocked the chain, opened the door a fraction more, tried to hide the room behind me with my body. She held out a book. Gray, with blue letters. I felt faint. "Here," she said. "This is my book. I want you to have it."

I took the book, but could not speak. Her book. *She was giving me her book.* She had told me once, when I handed in a report, *"You can be a writer."*

I was unable to do anything but cling to the door to keep from falling, and to keep her from seeing inside. I read the words on the cover: DARK WAS THE WILDERNESS–BY DOROTHY DUNN. I looked up at her face. When I did not speak, she said, "I know what will happen to you when you grow up."

"What?" It was my first word, and my last.

"I won't tell you now, but come and find me when you are grown, and I will tell you if I was right."

And she turned, and went back down the stairs.

When I was in my thirties, and had a libretto performed by Phyllis Byrn Julson, Robert Shaw, and the Atlanta Symphony in Carnegie Hall, I wrote to the Saint Louis Board of Education and asked for the address of Dorothy Dunn. They said she died within five years of the day she had knocked on my apartment door.

2

A dream uninterpreted is a letter unopened.
TALMUD

WHEN I was past fifty, in the week following the death of my mother, I dreamed that my lost grandmother — my father's mother — spoke to me. The image was a woman's upper body, middle aged, a little overweight. Her hair was short. I had no conscious memory of this woman. All that I knew about her was my mother's litany: she was poor, she was illiterate, she had had a nervous breakdown. I did not even know her name. Nevertheless, in the dream she appeared clearly, and the single sentence she spoke in the dream was so clear, so simple and so surprising, I woke with the memory as if someone in my waking life had actually said the words: *"What I have to offer you is Native American."*

Never had such a thing been suggested to me. I discounted the dream.

The next day my daughter called. She was in graduate school, working on an essay for an academic anthology that required an analysis of the work of a Native American performance group called Spiderwoman. She was struggling with her task, as she later stated, "How could a white woman begin to write about a Native American performance group in a way that grapples honestly and productively with the tangle of issues involved across difference?"

Rebecca was about to tell her editor that she could not complete the assignment, when on the same night as my dream, she felt a strange presence in her room, unlike anything she had experienced before, standing beside a Spiderwoman poster on the wall. "I had no idea who this absent presence was," Rebecca later wrote in her book, *The Explicit Body*. "I had no idea what she wanted. I felt I must be overtired, stressed out. I tried to ignore her, ignore my fear, and sleep. By then, as suddenly as I'd become aware of her presence, I became aware of her identity: she was my mother's father's mother."

All that Rebecca knew of her great grandmother was that she was an Ozark mountain woman. "Unable to deal with the invisible body, I decided to go downstairs, watch TV, and get real. What appeared on the screen was a PBS documentary about Ozark mountain women. I went back to bed. *What do you want?* The ghost told me to keep working. Then she was gone. The next day I called my mother on the phone."

FOUR months later I was packing to go to Ireland to lead a second year of creative writing workshops. In the pressure and busyness of my life, I had forgotten all about the dream. Máire, my Irish friend, was committed to using our one week of vacation together to drag me to old cemeteries in search of some English ancestors of mine who lived in Ireland. I had resisted her efforts to do that the previous year, and had no intention of doing it this time. I had read Leon Uris' *Trinity;* I was in love with Ireland, and I wanted no part of dead old English ancestors buried there.

I was in my office, packing books and materials for my Irish workshop, when it occurred to me that everyone has, after all, two grandmothers. And I didn't even know the name of one of mine. What if my father's mother had been named O'Brien or O'Toole! What if she were Irish! That would be a fine joke on Máire, an Irish Catholic nun who was bent on demonstrating her broad-mindedness by being terribly civilized about accepting my English forebears who had lived in Ireland, and treating me like a child of the old sod even though I could not boast a single drop of Irish blood.

The year had been intense for me; my mother had died, my last child had left for college, I was experiencing the hot flashes and insomnia of menopause. In June, as I was getting ready to leave, the dream of the preceding February no longer existed in my mind.

What was my grandmother's name?

My mother divorced my father after five years of marriage, when I was four years old. She had good reasons, and most of them were other women. After the divorce, she never let him come near my younger brother or myself, and she made me promise I would never see him or his people. I grew up hating him. Acutely. What she told me about his family was curt: they were poor white trash, and worse from her point of view, they were "ignorant." His mother could not read or write her own name. She signed her name with an "X." She had had a breakdown, and had been in a mental hospital for a year and a half. His father, Harv, was "just no good." Her refrain to close the matter ended — again and again — "I've never told you this before. Never tell anyone this. Harv had a child by his own retarded daughter! They're nothing but trash!" It was one of the deepest imprints of my childhood, varied sometimes with warnings like, "They'll be a noose around your neck!" And the final words, always, were *"Never, never have anything to do with them."*

Always I responded, "I promise, Mama."

He telephoned once. I was fourteen, Mama was at work. It was night; his words, *"Hello, Patsy? This is your Daddy,"* ricocheted off my conscious mind like an explosion. I had not heard his voice since I was four years old. But Mama's training was perfectly in place. Before he had a chance to say another word, I said, "The only Father I have is in Heaven." And hung up on him.

Mama praised me when she got home from work. "The damn fool," she said. "He was drunk. He called me earlier in the day. He wanted money."

I have no idea whether or not that was true. It could have been.

In my early forties I had visited an old friend in Missouri, and she urged me to at least find out if my father was still alive. She sat beside me and held one of my hands as I picked up the telephone receiver. The taboo was still so strong I was shaking as I dialed the operator in Waynesville, where he had lived, and asked if there was a listing for Cleve Vogt. I was given a number. It was his wife who answered. When I asked to speak to Cleve, she said in a voice that seemed to me to hold fear, "*He's been dead for five years.*"

I hung up quickly, then wondered how it might feel to a woman whose husband has been dead five years, to have a strange woman call for him by his first name. I felt compassion for her, and dialed the number again. I introduced myself: "I'm Cleve's oldest daughter, Pat." After a moment's silence, she said in a slow, merciless drawl, "*It sure did hurt your Daddy, to think you never came to see him.*"

I was outraged. It felt like a blow to the belly. In one minute of time I had learned that the father I lost at age four was dead, and that I was somehow guilty. But on the phone I was polite, civilized, controlled. Later I realized that in my gut I wanted to yell, *What?! He left me when I was four years old! Why didn't he ever come to see me? I was a child, for godssake!*

I said nothing of the kind. I said "thank you," and hung up. Two years later, when I wrote to "Mrs. Cleve Vogt, Waynesville, Mo." asking for a picture of him, she was kind. She sent it with a little note signed simply, "Hilda."

Wake Up Laughing

He was a young man in army uniform. A formal picture, a handsome young soldier. It was familiar — the only picture of him I had ever seen before. Even though I had been very young when I saw it, it was printed indelibly on my mind, because when I saw it before, at age five, it was on fire, burning in the hands of my mother, who was saying to me, "Your daddy sent you a picture. You want to burn this up, don't you? He never loved you. He has another little girl now. You want to burn the picture, don't you?" I remember nodding, "Yes." I remember fire on the face of my father.

As I packed for Ireland, I counted: twelve years had passed since I called Hilda to ask for my father's photograph. I had written many poems, many journal entries. I had done a lot of healing of old wounds. I had a granddaughter of my own. *What was my grandmother's name?*

I dialed information for the operator in Waynesville. In a slow, familiar southern Missouri accent, she gave me the number still listed under Cleve Vogt.

Hilda's "hello" was typical of country Missourians, especially in midsummer. I remember my mother's people saying "hello" the same way; it is a kind of snarl, as if you are expecting the worst, as you might say hello to a wasp in your sleeping bag.

"Hello," she said.

"Hello," I answered. "Is this Hilda?"

It was. I told her my name, and assuming she had forgotten, I reminded her as clearly and cheerfully as I could that I was her dead husband's first child. Hearing from me, I am certain, was not her idea of a perfect way to start a Saturday afternoon, but Hilda was remotely polite.

I told her quickly that I was just calling to ask for the name of my grandmother. That my mother had died in February, and my children (I lied) would like to know the name of their grandfather's mother. Could she please tell me her name. "Lakey," she said, leaning into the "a," elongating it, and lifting the final syllable as if half in question. "Elzina Lakey."

Damn! I thought, still bent on my hope of laughing at Máire, telling her I had an Irish grandmother. Lakey doesn't sound Irish. It probably comes from English "lake country." Another Brit!!

Then I said, "Lakey. Do you happen to know what nationality that name is?" I was standing at my desk, intending this to be as short a conversation as possible.

"No!" she said sort of like an expletive, and spit out, "All I know's she had Indian blood in her."

"*Indian* blood?" I asked.

"Yeah," she said. "But that's all I know." There was a long pause, in which I felt disoriented, wondered if she could mean Indian as in India, and sat down because I felt a growing vertigo. Then she added, "Leona might know more, I don't know."

I said, "Who's Leona?"

"Cleve's sister. The only one left."

That was as much information as I could assimilate at that moment. It had not occurred to me that he might have a living sister. I said thank you, that I would call Leona, and she gave me the phone number. I hung up the telephone receiver and sat unmoving. It was as if something seen out of focus through a lens slowly comes clear with the turning of the shaft in which the lens is set. The February dream came back to me. *"What I have to offer you is Native American."*

I stood, paced, and said out loud, *"Oh, my God!"*

Before I dialed Leona's number, I did some figuring in my head. She could be well past seventy years of age. I pictured her in a small house near Highway 66, the main artery through Missouri when I was a child. I imagined dark hair, a clean table with a cloth. Herself in a dark dress and an apron. I prepared myself to speak clearly and slowly, to give her time to process surprising information.

Leona said hello not so much in a snarl of anticipation of something bad, as in the weary acceptance of its having already happened.

Carefully, slowly, I said, "This is Cleve's oldest daughter, Pat."

There was silence on the other end of the line.

I said, "I am calling you because I would like to have some information about my father's mother. Your mother. I've just talked to Hilda, and she says my grandmother's name was Elzina Lakey."

She started to tell me, "Yes, that's right, that's—" then she stopped. I waited, and she said with absolute incredulity, "Why, is this *Patsy?*"

A N D there it was again — my childhood name in the dialect in which I first learned to speak. The slow lingering on the vowel sound; the gentle slur. Leona's voice was warm, rich with welcome. I have not answered to that name since I was a child, but I said yes, and she replied slowly, with obvious joy, "Why, *hon*, I haven't seen you since you was a little bitty thing!" She said "thing" as if it were "thaing," and let it slide slowly, lingering as if she were seeing the "thaing" that I was. "Why, I have a picture of you when you was just a little bitty *thaing!*"

We talked, then, about Elzina Lakey. Leona said yes, it was true, she "had Indian blood in her." I asked her if she knew what tribe, and she laughed, and said "No, I don't know nothing about that! My daughter says it's Cherokee, but I don't know." Lakey, she said, was the Indian name. I did not mention the dream. Well, I thought, "Lakey" doesn't sound Indian to me. I told her I was leaving for Ireland in two days, but I would write to her when I came back home. And already I knew that I wanted to go back to Missouri.

3

I R E L A N D that year was not about what I thought it would be about. I was invited for the second year to lead a writing workshop in a convent in Sligo. I had gone the year before, had entered the massive stone fortress of the Ursuline order that now held only a dozen nuns, most of them elderly. They had written stories of their childhood and youth; stories of entering the door of the convent as teen-agers who could never go home again even if a parent died; stories of the painful changes when Vatican II opened the cloistered communities and made no longer mandatory the ancient habits, the traditional ways.

I was going again. I expected the trip to Ireland to be about the Sisters, their stories, their memories. That did happen, but much more occurred that I did not expect.

I had almost no experience of Catholicism, and I was in flight from my own Protestant background. I had left the church forever; the pain of that divorce had not even begun to heal.

M Y mother was a self-taught intellectual. Her father had been an atheist who lived among fundamentalists. He read Darwin. He questioned everything, refused to conform to the attitudes of his neighbors. He found

13
Wake Up Laughing

a bundle of sticks on his front porch, the warning of the Ku Klux Klan, after he opened his country store one night to give patent medicine to black people. They had been turned away by the country doctor, who snarled through his screen door, "I don't doctor niggers!"

Mama was never at home with fundamentalism, and she was proud of her father's attitude toward black people, but her father was a tyrant, always right, always violently opposed to religion. She was converted as a young woman, hid some Sunday clothes behind a tree beside the road, and when her father wasn't looking, walked away from home, changed clothes, and went to the Methodists to be baptized. She preferred the Baptists, she said, but they wouldn't baptize her unless she became a member, and she didn't want to disobey her father that much. He found out about it later anyway, and yelled at her until her mother finally said "Richard, leave her alone." Mama said it was the only time in her life she ever heard her mother stand up to her father. Grandpa said he'd rather see Mama in her grave than a Christian.

She wanted me to have religion, but couldn't bring herself to take me to the local Baptist church, or even across the gravel road to the open air tabernacle at Mount Zion where we lived when I was five. I played around the tabernacle, though, and loved the singing, the sweet, narcotic pull of the gospel hymns: *Just as I am, without one plea,/ But that Thy blood was shed for me,/ And that Thou bid'st me come to Thee,/ Oh Lamb of God, I come. I come.*

I began to beg her to let me be "saved." She put me off, said "Some day. When you're older." I pulled daily on the hem of her dress and said, "Now, Mama. Now."

She told me later that she didn't know what to do. She believed I was too young to know what I was doing, but I was so insistent. Finally she took me out under one of the two scraggly peach trees in our "orchard," and told me just to pray, ask God to forgive my sins, and to say that I wanted to give my heart to Jesus. She laughed as she told me later, "You were so little! And you cried out there like a hardened criminal!"

What I remember is kneeling, and the branch of the peach tree above me, and one hard little peach alone on the whole tree. I remember a strange, sweet sense of a presence beyond the physical plane hearing me, accepting me, and looking upon me with delight.

PERSONAL ADDRESS

To you only I speak,
although you are forever
changing names, places
of residence, appearance,
affect. Reputation.

When I was a child
you hovered in the rafters
of the tabernacle, above
the visiting evangelist's head.
My mother said I should repent,
and so I did. Of what,
I have forgotten. I was
five years old. I do remember
how the tree, under which she knelt
and prayed with me for my salvation,
bore a single peach that year:
the hard, green bud of it. How
all the summer long I watched it grow.

There was something that I asked of you

in that worn-out orchard.
Although I don't remember what it was
I asked, I do know
I took the peach for answer.

Whatever that experience was, the only context I had in which to understand it was fundamentalist Christianity. My mother feared fundamentalism, but she had no opportunity to replace it with a broader theological understanding. She used the language of "salvation" but could not bear the actual churches that preached it, and tried to steer me toward a more middle ground. In order to do that, she talked about the Methodist church, although she never took me there. "They may not have as much spirit as the fundamentalists," she said to me, "but they aren't the little stingin' kind." By that she meant the judgment, the narrowness, the exclusiveness of the Holiness people at Mount Zion, the religious community to which she fled when she divorced my father. There I sat under great oak and hickory trees in the evenings at the edge of tent meeting revivals, listening as country people sang, *He's the lily of the valley, the bright and morning star, / He's the fairest of ten thousand to my soul* . . . The most beautiful, sensual, harmony I will ever hear, with lightning bugs like jewels twinkling between the trees.

We were country people, and I drank in that country religion. When I was eleven, after several attempts to make a living elsewhere, my mother moved us to St. Louis. Times were so hard that she soon decided she could not cope with my brother and me, and placed us in an orphanage in a wealthy community, a suburb of the tired old city where she lived in two rooms on third floor of a tenement. I had never attended church until the regularity of life in the orphanage made it possible. Possible even, to join a congregation.

• • •

Pat Schneider

Y O U are twelve years old. You think you are grown, but you are not. You are a child. Today is the day you have been waiting for — the day you will join the Methodist Church. June sunlight streams in through the windows of the gray stone church. Outside, the lawn is perfectly manicured, the shrubs are lush and green, not at all like the dirt yard of the Methodist church in the city, where your mother lives.

• • •

You do not know anyone here very well. The only time you can get to the church is on Sunday mornings, when someone from the congregation picks you up at the orphanage and drops you off there after the service. You know that the other twelve-year-olds who are joining the church have family here. Never mind. You know they are all families with money. Never mind. You look OK.

What are you wearing? Did the kind woman in the office at the orphanage help you choose a dress for this day? Never mind. Never mind.

You have wanted this. There is no father in the pew, watching you, but never mind. You have Father God. There is no mother sitting there being proud of you, but never mind. You have Mother Church. And you are coming home to them, and nobody knows you are different. See, your hair was curled last night with bobby pins you put in. Your shoes are shined. Your dress is OK. Nobody knows. You have passed. You are passing.

The minister in his black robe comes down to the altar. He calls the confirmation class forward. You all go — seven twelve-year-olds line up, their backs to the congregation. He says the words of invitation; you respond in unison with the others: I do. I do. I will. And then he tells the group to turn and face the congregation. He comes down the row introducing each child. You are the next to last in the line. When he comes to you, he says, "This is Pat. She is very special. She comes to us from Edgewood Children's Home."

You don't hear anything more. You don't understand your feelings. You know you are special. You know the people will pay more attention to you, be

Wake Up Laughing

kinder, because of his words. He is being kind; he wants people to pay attention to you. But you want to disappear. You want to go backwards to this morning before you came to the church, or at least backwards to just before he called you forward, when you were still just yourself before God, a worshipper in the congregation like all the others.

Maybe you had forgotten you came from Edgewood. You go back to the pew. You stand with the congregation to sing, and the church disappears. God doesn't disappear; the church disappears, and God comes in close. Father. Mother. You sing, and you know that the song was chosen for you and for you alone: Oh love, that will not let me go . . .

> Oh love, that will not let me go,
> I rest my weary soul in thee,
> I give thee back the life I owe,
> that in thine ocean depths its flow
> may richer, fuller be.
>
> Oh joy, that seekest me through pain,
> I dare not ask to fly from thee,
> I trace the rainbow through the rain
> and feel the promise is not vain
> that morn shall tearless be.

• • •

A YEAR and a half later, I returned to my mother. The church, a few blocks from Sarah and Olive Streets where we lived, was a tired old building and a weary congregation unable to adapt to the changing class and ethnic diversity of the neighborhood. Nevertheless, I took it for anchor, harbor, haven from the chaos of home.

I was a senior in high school when the minister told me one Sunday morning that it was important for me to come to youth group that evening. I nodded yes, but I couldn't go. The Sunday evening a week before there had been a potluck meal for the high school group, and we had nothing in our two rooms suitable to take to a potluck. I had wanted to go, badly, and my mother said she would make some cranberry sauce; she was sure that would be fine. We lived on balogna sandwiches made with puffy white bread, hot dogs, canned peas. Nothing was ever really cooked, just cans opened, contents warmed up and eaten usually standing, since all the chairs in the two rooms were piled with dirty clothes, clutter. There were no closets, no dressers. But for some reason that day she had cranberries. She had sugar.

My mother was not a cook. The "cranberry sauce" was runny, sour, embarrassing. I went, anyway, hoping the sauce would pass for potluck. But it didn't. No one took more than one bite, and I decided I would never go again.

In the week after the missed meeting, Rev. Harris knocked on my door. This was the worst thing that could happen. There was nothing I could do; I let him in, shoved clutter aside, asked him to sit down. He told me that he had wanted me at the youth group because they had planned a party for me — and they were going to tell me that the church would pay my way through college. Someone had died and left money to the church; he had convinced the congregation to give it to me as scholarship instead of applying it to the building fund. I tried to act surprised. In fact, I was surprised, but not at what he might have expected. I was surprised that it cost money to go to college. It hadn't cost money to go to high school. It had not dawned on me until that moment how perilously close I had come to the end of my educational way.

Rev. Harris was a good man, and he certainly saved my sanity if not my life. During the first two years of college I would come home in agony of spirit, begging him to help me save my own belief in the virgin birth, my uncompromising loyalty to the literal text, my confidence in the dogmas of fundamentalism. He was gentle. He did not burden me with the fact, later understood, that he himself didn't believe in those things. Rather, he gently assured me that if I just used my own mind, I would be all right.

In college, however, my religion professor took as his mission the destruction of the young literalists who came to his classroom, and there were plenty of us in that "Bible Belt" small town college. He pointed out inconsistencies in the Biblical texts, textual variants, incongruities, things impossible to literally believe. In no time at all, I "got it." My faith didn't make sense. I suffered a traumatic loss of belief in the literal text, which means to a fundamentalist a loss of personal orientation, a loss of an intimate, personal relationship with Jesus. It is an eternal loss. I felt everything was in fog. I no longer knew who Jesus was, or what to believe in. The only thing that was unshaken was that original sense of Presence. Everything else was gone. I was desperate, and was devastated when Rev. Harris and his wife were killed; a train struck their car at an unmarked railroad crossing.

I changed to another school, thinking I would somehow get back my lost faith in the virgin birth and with it a full system of belief. But the professor of Bible there also pointed to the inconsistencies, the impossibilities of literalism. He did so, however, with joy, excitement and a far deeper spirituality. He helped me to see my own change as a beginning rather than as an end. I read *I and Thou* by Martin Buber and saw that everything is holy. Everything is sacred text. For the first time I knew what I wanted to do with my life: be a teacher, a professor, who would teach Old Testament and New Testament on the college level. I was in love with the ancient text; I knew long passages of the Hebrew poets by heart: Isaiah, Jeremiah, Amos, the Psalms:

> *Whither shall I go from thy Spirit?*
> *Or whither shall I flee from thy presence?*

Pat Schneider

If I ascend up into heaven, thou art there:
if I make my bed in hell, behold, thou art there.
If I take the wings of the morning,
And dwell in the uttermost parts of the sea;
even there shall thy hand lead me
and thy right hand shall hold me.
If I say, "Surely the darkness shall cover me,"
even the night shall be light about me.

It was such a relief to understand that I didn't have to protect those beloved texts any more by clinging to literal interpretations. I had broken the bonds of fundamentalism, and was ready to prepare myself to teach the Bible as I wished it had been taught to me when I first entered college.

But when I appeared at Pacific School of Religion (PSR) to claim the scholarship they offered me, I was told that I could not receive any degree except a master's degree in religious education, a degree that would prepare me to administer Sunday Schools for children in local churches — *because I was a woman.*

Looking back at it from the distance of a life lived across the great divide of this century's awakening of women's consciousness, and across my own awakening, I am appalled at the passivity of my own acceptance of that institutional refusal. I don't think I even felt anger. PSR was one of the finest, most challenging theological seminaries in the United States; there was no better. I remember a kind of soggy disappointment; a sense that my own vocational "call" must somehow be inappropriate. I had thought my work would be important. But it would not. I would always be only a lackey, only a low-level helper to those who were the ministers, the leaders. I remember a turn toward the probability of marriage. This was not an attempt to marry a minister as a vicarious substitute for my own professional identity. It was a much deeper struggle, an attempt —

brutal, on the psychological level — to convince myself that being a "helpmate" to a man could be my calling, to believe that for me, "wife" alone could become itself a calling, a vocation. It was the middle of the 1950s in America. It was what I was supposed to believe.

I took courses that were not necessary for my degree, in theology and in Old and New Testament studies — courses that filled me with intense excitement. But on some deep level I gave up my own sense of vocation.

By the time I took my final exam I was married to Peter, a young minister with whom I thought I could form a partnership serving churches. And I was nine months pregnant with the first of our four children. On the way home from the exam, I waddled downtown, bought a print of Vermeer's "The Milkmaid," took it home and hung it above our dining table as a reminder to myself that my professional life was no longer that of the mind, but of the body. I tried to celebrate it. I lived with that picture on my wall until we left the church, twenty-five years later. All the while I was working as a mother, a minister's wife. I wrote plays and libretti, but they were for the church, trying to call the church to deeper awareness of social justice. On the personal and emotional level I tried to be *nothing but* the woman in the painting: a woman at a table pouring a stream of sweet milk out of a pitcher into a bowl.

The last church we served was in Amherst, Massachusetts, a university and college town. As I remember those days, they are clouded with the pain of the loss of innocence in my country and in myself: the death of John Kennedy had already happened. During our years there, Robert Kennedy and Martin Luther King were assassinated, students at Kent State were gunned down, and more than ten thousand students marched past our church building from the University of Massachusetts campus to the common in the center of town, protesting the war. A student came into the sanctuary, cut up the American flag and placed the shredded cloth on the altar. A Baptist minister to students set himself on fire on the campus in protest to the war, and died in flames. When President Nixon ordered the bombing of Cambodia on Christmas eve, Peter called from the pulpit for his impeachment.

Against the backdrop of that national upheaval we began to dream a different sort of church than the traditional model, a dream that would ultimately bring us into conflict with the church hierarchy.

I will come back to that. For now it is enough to say that before my first trip to Ireland Peter and I left the church completely, knowing that we would never return. We were both suffering in the months that followed that decision. We left our lifetime vocation at ages fifty and forty-seven with no idea of how we were going to survive. We had always lived in furnished parsonages; we had no bed, no table, no chairs. We had an eight year old child still at home, a son graduating from high school and two daughters in college. We worked furiously to try to make ends meet financially, cashing in our small clergy retirement in order to survive.

I tried to write about what was happening to me. One poem about leaving the church went through thirty-seven drafts. Instinctively trying for a tighter and tighter form to hold the chaos I felt breaking around and within me, I rhymed both ends of the lines, struggling for some way to order my confusion and loss.

LETTING GO

As a beggar, resting in the sun,
Peels off layers of her outer rags,
Astonished to discover that each one
Reveals another under it, her paper bags

Filling with the garments she had worn
When everything was harder, darker, colder;
As she feels the chill of being born
Again, wiser now, and older,

Wake Up Laughing

> So I. Having shed the church in the belief
> That one particular chill of letting go
> Might be a kind of ultimate relief,
> (A flat sun of contradiction, saying "No"
>
> To winter, to the ice around the heart,)
> Under vestments I am finding near the skin
> Ragged garments where all distinctions start.
> I blunder toward the person I had been
>
> Before costuming for the beggar's part
> And trying out in someone else's show.
> Living now is nakedness of heart;
> Dying — just another letting go.

Four years after leaving the church, I was exhausted and in personal despair. The pressures of survival had brought pressure on our marriage. I was in every way in crisis, and I thoroughly disliked myself. I went alone for a week of silent retreat at a place called Isabel's House behind a monastery near Gloucester, Massachusetts. In a Catholic retreat center, one is expected to receive some direction from the retreat leader. I told Isabel, the nun who ran the retreat house, that I was a Protestant, I was confused, and I didn't want to talk to anyone or have anyone talk to me. I asked her if I could stay, anyway, and she said yes. I had been for four years out of the church after a lifetime of constant music, liturgy, community. I had been long enough away that I no longer sang the hymns to myself, nor did I, in words at least, pray. At the end of my retreat, I wrote these words in my journal:

> I was walking on the beach on the next to last day of retreat, walking among great stones at low tide, troubled. I found myself

saying, "The world speaks in sign language, and everything is a sign." I did not seem to have the thought before the words came out of my mouth; I seemed, rather, to hear the thought from my own lips for the first time. After a while, walking, picking up small amber and white snail shells, it occurred to me that I was saying those words over and over, over and over, and that it seemed each time I said them I would find a piece of beach glass.

I laughed at my own foolishness and tried to forget such an idea. But I couldn't get it out of my consciousness, and I was finding an unbelievable number of pieces of green, white and aqua polished glass among the shells. I vowed I would not put it to the test, and did not — but the words kept rising, and the glass kept tinkling into my pocket. On the way back to my room I remembered with some relief that the day before had been stormy, for the first time in ten days of retreat there had been real surf — that surely explained the fact that there was so much more beach glass than there had been on my previous walks. Although I love the gentle colors of beach glass, and see it always as a kind of unconscious art form, mending the break between wilderness and civilization, on this day I had been primarily collecting shells — particularly the tiny amber ones and the white spiraled snail shells, most especially those that were broken, laying open the ivory perfection of their inner chambers.

On the last day I began my walk truly having forgotten the chant of the day before; I was still wrestling with myself in my mind. Then, as if by some internal rhythm, the words came, "The world speaks in sign language, and everything, everything is a sign." And at my feet, a piece of beach glass.

I can only say that this reached ridiculous proportions on the walk. It was so absolutely obvious: the inner voice, the chant, and then the shining piece of polished glass, that it became funny; I began to talk to the world out loud — to say, "You are communicating with me, aren't you — and everything is a sign, isn't it?" I continued finding among the shells, gold, white, lovely broken shells, glowing bits of beach glass, feeling an increasingly ecstatic sense of language — of being addressed — until the crescendo of joy became so great I was laughing and almost running from piece to piece of colored glass — three or four at a time, saying "alright, alright, I understand. I do think I understand! I have thought only certain things were a 'sign,' — the fool hot air balloons in summer over my house at home, surprising me with their comic huffs, their magic silence; the black-eyed Susan blooming high up in the shelter of a limb of the maple tree in my neighbor's yard — and maybe the words of Jesus, and Isaiah. — Until now, I have selected certain things and recognized them as 'signs,' but everything is a sign."

I picked up a wonderful long crystal of white, ocean-polished glass, and an arch of green, and said to the world, "I get it! Now you can stop giving me these jewels, if you want to!"

Then, being human, and a little stupid, I pronounced to the clutter of glory under my feet, "This is so simple, and so obvious, and so important; all that is required is loving the world — and receiving each detail, each moment, each object as sign. As long as I live, I will —" And I started to make a vow, a promise . . .

But the voice in my head, replying, was cool, and weary, and very explicit. "Oh, don't. Don't do that. Don't go making an idol of this experience. A dogma. Don't."

And there, as if in final blessing, just where the lip of the ocean moved, touching the sand, there was a perfect ball of glass. I guess it was a child's marble, lost on the beach, washed, softened into sea glass by the ocean — but it might as well have been the round earth, given into my hand. I walked back to my room in Isabel's

House without finding another piece of beach glass. Nor did I need one.

Later that last night, sitting in the window watching the sun go down over the ocean, I became aware of a gull that was behaving differently from any of the hundreds of gulls I had watched during the week. She was sitting placidly on the water directly in front of my window, facing me. Suddenly she winged herself straight up into the air about three or four feet and plummeted back, head straight down, just submerging herself and then surfacing, arranging her feathers, and was again poised on the water facing me. She wasn't fishing; I'm certain of it. She was either bathing (although she didn't seem to be working with her feathers as barnyard birds do when they clean themselves) or she was playing. She repeated this spasm of energy, up, down, serene, eight or ten times. I think she was playing.

I sat watching, thinking, "What is this a sign of? What does it mean?" and almost articulated something pompous to myself about universal humor — but caught myself, and didn't. Mercifully, I let it go, for the first time in my life perceiving that I, myself, am a sign. I don't need a translation. I can speak the language; the world speaks sign language. Sometimes it is a sign of nothing but the astonishing fact of itself — taken literally.

ISABEL was a beautiful woman. The spirit of the woman was visible in her face: warm, and rich, and without pretense. She knelt in her garden behind her house, working with plants. Her artificial leg lay near her on the ground. She told me, that week, that she had a virus of some sort. A year later, when I called to see if I could return, I was told she had died of cancer. I did not hear her name again until several years later, in Ireland, when I was told there would be three women coming to my workshop from "Isabel's House," outside Dublin, a house named for "an American nun," that offers educational assistance to women in economic stress. Very much, I was told, like my own work leading free writing workshops for women in public housing projects in the Connecticut River valley where I live.

Four years after my silent retreat in Gloucester, I was invited for the first time back to Pacific School of Religion as a writer, and as a teacher of creative writing. I had found my way into a profession. Both my writing and my teaching of writing gave me enormous satisfaction. My play, *Berries Red*, began my exploration of childhood poverty and the complicated story of leaving the church that saved me from that poverty. I used for transitions between scenes of adult life, several old hymns that had been my survival in childhood. They were used for irony now, as well as for sweet memory. Juxtaposing them with radical oppositions, I made the actress struggle to remember lines: *He's the lily of the valley, the bright and morning star/ the fairest of ten thousand to my soul . . .*

Now my play would be produced at the very school that had denied my professional vision when I was young. I would stand with gray hair teaching in the very rooms where I sat as a student longing to teach and was told I could not, because I was a woman. Much more problematically, I would teach people whose eagerness and enthusiasm for the church equaled what my own had been.

But I had changed.

• • •

The campus is a patch of green perched so high up in the Berkeley hills you can feel vertigo just standing at the end of the sidewalk at night where the earth drops into dark streets and the roofs of houses, and far, far out along the edges of the world and on the other side of water are the lights of San Francisco and the lights of Marin County connected by a filament, a web of light that is the Golden Gate Bridge. It hurts, it is so beautiful, and so you turn your back on it, and that doesn't help because in front of you now is a straight walk dividing an expanse of grass between buildings you love — shadowy but clear they are there, all the way to the end of the walk where the deliberate, unequivocal stone library stands on the left and the chapel on the right. Beyond them is the dark street falling away to Euclid Avenue and then the hill rising against the night sky, prickling with lights as near as San Francisco is distant. You catch your breath. This is the spot where you walked at night with Casey, roommate, friend, fiercely brilliant young woman. And Casey is dead, and what is "dead?" — doesn't she stand just there — there — just inside the shadow of the trees against the chapel? And doesn't she sit there, on the stone steps, her back to you, looking over to San Francisco?

This is the place. Is it the time? This is the place where you said you would marry, and Peter is over there, right there, on the steps, too, with his black hair crew cut, and his life set toward being a pastor. There is the anticipation of new babies in his hands, the palm of his right hand wet with the baptismal water, his voice rich and deep in the sanctuary, his voice singing with the congregation the words of his favorite hymn: "He who would valiant be 'gainst all disaster/ Let him with constancy, follow the Master/ Nor ever once relent his first avowed intent/ To be a pilgrim."

The night is sweet with the smell of fruit trees in bloom, and it is only February. Somewhere there is Massachusetts and snow. Somewhere there is a time when the ministry is a closed and locked room. Somewhere there is a place where Casey has died and your own children have been born and have grown up and moved out into another, a different world.

But here, now, you swim in stars that are not stars at all, and you breathe the sweet breath of your loves and hear the words of the old songs, and oh! this is why we aren't allowed to go back, and oh! this is why we aren't allowed to know tomorrow.

• • •

I had asked the administration to limit my workshop to twelve participants. I arrived at the door to the classroom to discover twenty-four men and women, all looking at me, registered and expectant. My first words to them were "Wait here — I'll be right back." I left the room, went to the Director's office. She said she was certainly sorry — they had no idea the course would be so popular.

Two days later, I walked across campus in an internal whirlwind of feelings; overwhelmed with twice as many people as I came prepared to lead; my exercises, my handouts, my plans, inadequate. And the personal history that was crashing on the shores of my mind. Coming toward me was the tall, young Irish woman who was in my workshop. I liked her grin. Instinctively, I trusted her, but at that moment she was one of twenty-four — interesting, but unknown.

We stopped, and she leaned closer to me, and said something like *"Pat, I know there are more of us than you expected, but I just want to tell you, it is going very well."* And the wall of my self-protection cracked, and I broke; I couldn't stop, I poured out my relief to have someone speak personally to me; I poured out my own inner turmoil, secrets of my soul, struggles of my personal life, that I certainly had no conscious intention of pouring forth, and I am certain she had no expectation of receiving!

She invited me to dinner, and then, because I would find out anyway if I was coming to her apartment, she told me she was a Roman Catholic nun.

In disguise, I thought to myself. I was as shocked at that moment as she must have been when I poured out a torrent of confession upon her, unasked. I think now that at that moment I felt a little trapped. The last thing I wanted was to be "ministered unto"! It would seem very rude to turn down the dinner invitation, and it would leave the sudden intimacy raw at the edges. For lack of any wiser choice, I accepted the invitation, went to dinner with Máire, (pronounced *moy-rah*) and another Sister, had a chance to hear some of Máire's story. She was newly returned from many years in Africa; she went with the food trucks to villages where people were starving, held an emaciated baby as it died. Life in Africa had been at the edge, somehow; she was nervous about returning to the Ursuline Convent in Ireland. And then we went on with the week of intense workshop. I don't remember having another private conversation.

Before I left California, Máire said to me, "Come and visit me in Ireland." And I, thinking her suggestion was the most unlikely thing I had heard in my life, said, "And you come and visit me in Massachusetts."

But Máire *did* come to visit me in Massachusetts on her way back to Ireland. One day, without warning, she called from Boston and asked would I come pick her up for a wee visit. She had no idea that Boston was a four-hour round trip from Amherst. I said "of course," but it would take me a while to get there. Much later I learned that her awkwardness was symptomatic of the huge risk she was taking. She had never once stayed overnight in a private home since entering the convent at age seventeen.

When she arrived back in Sligo she wrote, saying if I could come I would be the guest of the convent, and my only expense would be my flight. In that same week, I received an invitation from my friend Rachel, a former member of my Amherst workshop, to visit her in Liverpool. Two in one week seemed something akin to a summons, and so I accepted the invitation, telling Máire that if I was going to be housed at the Convent's expense, I would be happy to give them a writing workshop in exchange, if they should want it.

That first year's experience in Ireland began with opening Leon Uris' *Trinity*, on the airplane as we lifted off from the Hartford, Connecticut airport. I read it all the way across the Atlantic, getting madder and madder at the English as I approached what they have called "The British Isles."

Máire picked me up at the airport in Sligo, and said, "I want to drive you around Sligo a little before I take you to the convent." Somewhere in

Wake Up Laughing

that first hour as we were making conversation, I mentioned that my mother told me I have Irish ancestors. She said, quick as a wink, "What are their names, love?"

As an American who had thought very little about Ireland in my life, I had no way of knowing the significance of that question. I blissfully, ignorantly, answered, "Let's see," trying to remember what my mother had told me, "I think there was "Mercer," and "Barrett" — I can't remember the others.

"English," she said.

I honestly didn't understand what she meant.

"They're *English* names, love. Can you remember any other names?"

I felt shock, and some pain; not that I had very much invested in having Irish ancestors — the information that there might be some had come to me from my mother as I was preparing for my trip. Years before, to please her, I had taken her suitcases full of genealogical notes and made a book of it. It was clear that it was a history of "her family." Neither my mother nor I ever mentioned "my family," half of which was, genealogically speaking, erased. My mother was in her early eighties. I took her book with me to please her, and said if I was in the neighborhood, I would take a snapshot of the graves of "her" ancestors.

In afterthought, I know that the real point of shock, however, was instinctive and ancient. I thought I heard under Máire's words the familiar old pattern: *you live on the wrong side of the tracks!* In addition to personal history, instinctive and conscious, there was the fact that I was newly surfaced from Uris' bloody history — I had battering rams against cottages freshly imprinted on my mind, and before I was ten minutes on Irish sod, I was being told I was a child of the enemy!

Of course Máire, who hardly knew me (we had engaged in exactly two days of conversation) had no idea of the passion with which I received her information. My memory is that she said it two or three times into my stunned silence, and then I told her I didn't want to *talk about it any more right now,* and that I had absolutely no interest whatsoever in looking for the graves of dead English ancestors.

Whereupon Máire turned and looked at me for one meaningful moment, and changed into the ultimate sensitive nun. It was her mission to make me understand that Protestants were just fine with her. We were in the parking lot of the cemetery where William Butler Yeats is buried. She told me story after story about wonderful Protestant patriots, including Yeats, whose grave we approached and stood beside as if he could save us from this ohmygod immediate impasse. Unfortunately, the chapel at Yeats' grave site is full of flowery tributes to the Queen, that — sensitive nun or not — she could not help pointing out with two curt, meaningful words: *The Queen . . .*

Just about the time we reached the altar of the chapel, and the third or fourth Queenly mention, I said to myself, *Self, shut up. Just shut up and learn a thing or two. This has nothing whatever to do with you — you don't care about the damned ancestors, English or not, and you don't know a thing about this woman's history, so shut up and learn!* And suddenly everything was history, and none of it applied to me, and we were just fine, and I did begin to learn a thing or two.

When Máire invited me to go to Mass with her in Donegal, I went. The priest was young, beautiful, and very warm. There were a lot of people there — on a Wednesday! — and their piety moved me. I felt myself seduced into the old, familiar love. I was flowing in the river of blessing, I was at home. And then, the young priest lifted the chalice, held it high, and gave the invitation. It was as if someone slapped me across the face. *You damned fool,* I said to myself. *He's not inviting* you!"

I felt like I was staggering out of the church, I felt so much pain. And anger. Not "at Catholics" — at *myself,* for allowing myself to be seduced back into what I felt was a system of balderdash, a way of organizing the spirit to nonexistence, a way of keeping women down and men up, a way of keeping whoever Jesus was locked away, inaccessible, portioned out in little dry wafers by those with power to those without power.

To try to talk to Máire about it was impossible. It was hers; it was sacred to her. And it was beautiful; that's why it had "hooked" me. I said to myself, *Put it away. Like you put the English/Irish thing away, put this away. It doesn't have anything to do with you — you are in Máire's country, a guest in Máire's life. You are fortunate to be here, to be taken in with so much love. You don't know anything of what this is about. So shut up and learn something.* And I did, and everything was easy again. Máire and I stopped talking about religion.

FINALLY, safely armored against English-ness, Irish-ness, and church-ness, I enjoyed sightseeing. Máire took me to wonderful places in Donegal — we saw wild swans, wild yellow irises, hundreds of sheep (she called them "sheepeens") wild cliffs on the far side of Aran Isle, and her lovely Nellie, Eibhlín, Bríd and other family members.

It was on the last day of our time together that she took me to Dún Lúiche (Dunlewy), the little settlement nestled below Errigal, the mountain in whose shadow she had grown up. We had been talking for days, days, and a lovely silence had fallen between us. We had survived my intensities, and her own, and I think we were by that time very good friends. She knew where my sorest spots were, and I had discovered a couple of hers. We each were pretty good at being still when it was called for.

She took me to the most beautiful ruin of a church. It is high, and vast, and without a roof. It is stone, as was the church in St. Louis where I first gave my heart to the God of a church. My life to her service. My heart to her God. The sky was wonderful, and still. It was Ireland in the sunshine. Errigal rose above us on one side, the Devil's Glen rose sheer on another side, and far below we could see the sea. In the center of the valley, between mountain, cliff and sea, and exactly the color of outcropping rocks, was this most amazing ruined church.

We went through the gate, across a small stretch of grass, and into the arched doorway. We were silent. Máire stood back, and I advanced toward the space where once there had been an altar. All around were arched windows, the lead still criss-crossed across their empty space. It was breathtakingly beautiful to me. Behind me, very quietly, very gently, as if it were almost being laid down as an offering, Máire said, "Love, this is a Protestant church."

Suddenly I was in the stone church in St. Louis where I went by myself at thirteen, refugee from the two dirty rooms where I lived with my mother, my brother, and my mother's mother. Standing in the broken Irish church, the words of the hymn we sang every Sunday as the choir processed came up in me, and I began to sing it out loud, the grassy floor beneath me, the sky a roof above me, and around me the white stone walls with their windows still leaded, empty of glass, full of light. As I sang, the choir in wine-colored robes, their white collars, their navy-blue Methodist hymnals open in their hands, came up the aisle behind me and to my right. I stood in the third pew from the front, my own hymnal open in the palms of my two hands. At the back of the choir, Rev. Harris came in his black robe, singing. We all sang:

> *Holy, Holy, Holy, Lord God Almighty,*
> *Early in the morning, my song shall rise to Thee.*
> *Holy, Holy, Holy, merciful and mighty,*
> *God in Three Persons, blessed Trinity.*

Máire was silent as I sang, and as my singing broke into weeping. A lesser priest would have come toward me, would have put arms around me, would have come in to the solitary place where I stood. She did not move, did not whisper, and I sat down where once there had been an altar, and I saw: my grief had not been about being a minister's wife. It was not about the difficult and strange tangle of what my role was through those twenty-five years. It was not about Peter's relationship with the district superintendent and the bishop, nor his theology nor his sense of call. My grief had to do with a thirteen year old girl who gave her life to the church and her heart to *the holy one,* for whom she had no name other than "God in Three Persons, Blessed Trinity." "Father." "Mother Church and Father God." My grief had nothing to do with membership. Nothing to do with Pacific School of Religion. Nothing to do with Protestantism. It had to do with *the holy one.*

I always knew intellectually, but in that moment I knew in some deeper dimension, as if I myself were pure spirit, that the holy one cannot be held in a building with a roof. Here sheep wandered in and out of the sanctuary, wind blew through the leads where there had been stained glass, and a country girl grown up stood in the dignity of her profession, silently, as priest. Here in the silence I was met by the same indefinable Presence that had met me when I reached out in my mind at age five, in the worn-out orchard at Mount Zion. That presence was not fundamentalist, not Protestant, not Catholic, not Christian. There could be no roof, no defining doors closed around it. It was personal. It was holy.

THROUGHOUT the year between my first and second visits, Máire took upon herself the task of reconciling me with my English ancestors. This she did in spite of my categorical insistence that they did not interest me whatsoever. She did it sweetly. For instance, she sent me tapes of herself singing Irish folk songs. Máire O'Donohoe has a voice to break the heart, and if given the gift of a tape, one listens. Many times. And every time I listened, I got told, "Now, love, this is a song from the land of *your people.*" Meaning Northern Ireland. Meaning English settlements there. On one tape she waxed absolutely lyrical about the beauty of the "land of my people." And she made it perfectly clear that the following summer, we *were* going to go there.

It was a lovely time for me in Liverpool the previous year. Rachel is a fabric artist and a poet, and to my American eyes she is quintessentially British. I was cared for like royalty in her home, fed little homemade delicacies, given a hot-water bottle to take to bed. I felt as if I were wrapped around by Wordsworth: *trailing clouds of glory,* and Tennyson: *Our little systems have their day/ They have their day and cease to be. . .;* and Shakespeare, for goodness sakes: *Our little lives are rounded by a sleep* — England is interesting, no doubt about it. But I had no desire to have antique English ancestors pushed upon me when I was happily vegetating in my ignorance. I was single-minded in my sympathy for the Irish.

Máire was eloquent in her statements about her own lack of prejudice regarding people and things English; she went to great lengths to educate me on the wonderful English patriots who had fought for Irish independence, on her own family members who are Protestant, and on the good relations between Catholics and Protestants in Southern Ireland, *et cetera* and *ad nauseam*. But she also took me to a grotto where her Catholic forebears worshipped in secret in the days when Catholic Masses were illegal; I was shown crosses with short cross-beams that could be secreted up a priest's sleeve in case of sudden attack; I saw photos in national park centers of English landlords aiming battering rams at peasant cottages while Irish women and children looked helplessly on; and I listened many times to my tape of Máire's own voice sweetly singing songs of the resistance, songs of sorrow, songs of suffering. *She* may not be prejudiced, but after the short course that she and Leon Uris gave me in Irish history, *I* was prejudiced, and I wanted nothing to do with any English ancestors.

As far as my father's genealogy was concerned, all I knew at that time was that his name was Vogt, not the Vought of my mother's Anglicized re-spelling. I assumed that was German. My attempt to see if his lost mother might have had an Irish name had failed. And as far as my mother's genealogy — I pasted proudly across my heart the legend I read on the broken wall of a public building in the shadow of Sligo's majestic mountain, Ben Bulben: BRITS OUT!

But I knew, as I prepared to leave once more for Ireland in early June, that this very disciplined friend of mine had decided — for my own good, of course — that she would take me through the British barricades into the foreign land of her own nation's north, and there she would introduce to me to my ancestors, whether I wanted them or not. A nun's meekness, I have decided, is the meekness of a boa constrictor. Once you are embraced, you that know you are embraced.

• • •

We stopped just inside the town line at a small grocery store. "The old Quaker cemetery," Máire said, coming out from talking with the man behind his counter cluttered with Belfast and Dublin newspapers, ripe bananas, penny candy and Kodak film, "is behind the Castle Moat."

"The castle moat?" I asked, imagining a wide space of water, turrets, drawbridge.

"This town is Moat," Máire said patiently, kindly. "So the castle here is called 'the Castle Moat.'" She had by this time dealt with me long enough to be able to translate my confusion. "The Quaker cemetery is behind the castle," she said. There's just one old lady living in the castle by herself. She won't mind if we just push the big iron gates open and walk right through the castle yard. He says we'll see the cemetery wall out back."

It was exactly as he said. The tall, iron gates, the Castle Moat without a moat — without, in fact, turrets or towers or anything very castlelike, except size. Size, in this little town, the Castle Moat did have: a huge, ugly, rectangular stone house with a large yard, a high iron gate, and far back to the rear, an ancient-looking stone wall with another iron gate.

Pat Schneider

As we released the wire catch and pushed the first gate open, I was struck by fact: I am opening the gate to a castle. My body is moving across a green lawn beside a castle toward an old cemetery that I know was familiar over three hundred years ago to a Quaker man named Isaac Steer. My ancestor. There may well be bones of my ancestors mixed into the soil of this place. Beside me, an Irish nun turns to read my face. She is my friend. She is a country as foreign to me, and as familiar, as inevitable, as this castle, this gate, that overgrown stone wall in the distance, enclosing the graveyard named in Mama's book of genealogy. The place of lost, old English Quakers whom only yesterday, unless I opened that book, I could not name. And did not want to acknowledge.

She tries the second gate. "It's locked," I say with some relief. Beyond the gate we see a stone arch, overgrown with weeds, all that is left of a building, with inscriptions carved on either side of the arch. She hands me her car keys, grasps the iron bars, and swings herself high up over the top of the gate. I look up at her triumphant grin. "Can you make it?" she says. She is challenging me, my extra years of age. She is laughing at me. And there I am, skirt hoisted, two legs astraddle a high iron gate in County Meath, Ireland.

Oh, Máire, how do I find my way now with words — all that rich overgrowth and undergrowth — the nettles and the Queen Anne's lace, the miniature Ferris wheels, wheels within wheels, days turning to night, dreams of falling, dreams opening to day, prehistory guessed at in the ancient Irish stones, Celtic circles, spirals, the old stone arch entrance to an abandoned cemetery, broken archway, entrance to the place of — the place of — you say it for me, long before I can say it, long before I want to say it, like laying down a bridge across a castle moat, like riding up in a Ferris wheel toward the stars and gasping for the fear of earth lost, lost, — you say it for me; "Pat," you say, "the place of your people."

And I feel the child in me rise up. No! No! You have no ancestors except the fossils in the creek in your childhood. You do not belong on this side of the tracks! Don't listen! Don't try to cross over! Ancestors belong to people who have privilege and class! You will get hurt! You will be found out for what you are: poor, and dirty, and shameful! Remember who you are! Orphanage, only orphanage you will claim! Slum tenement alone will you recognize! No! People with history, people with ancestors — they are the enemy! They are the *"HAVES"* and you are from the *"HAVE NOTS!"* You will not, can not connect yourself to history, to the confusion of it, the brutality of it, the class struggles, the possibility of guilt, the old wars, the old prides. You will love only your own pain! You will honor only the angry child, the angry child! Remember the retreating form of the father, remember the quicksand need of the mother. It is the pain that has kept you safe, and the radical disconnection. Remember the disconnection; it is who you are! If you connect, then who you are — who you always have been — will disappear!

"Pat," you say. You say it again and again, delighted with yourself. "Pat, this is the place of your people."

"I don't want them," I tell you one last time. "They were English. Look what the English did to your ancestors. Look what they still do. Look at the blood. Look at the broken, abandoned houses. I remind you that you yourself named it: 'They are English names.'"

You climb before me up the iron gate. You go before me down into the nettles. You take my camera, you take your car keys. You are laughing at me in the midst of that complicated history: "Can you make it?" I am fifteen years older than you. Through the iron bars of the antique gate, you in the place of my people, me in the place of your people — the broken arch of a Quaker meeting house behind your head, the steeple of a distant Catholic church behind my head, suddenly you look like a child to me. Your face is set in a kid's grin; you are daring me to go forward into freedom, into joy. I swing myself up and over the gate. I would not take your hand for assistance if my life depended on it. I know a dare when I hear one. Coming down into the cemetery one small nettle brushes my leg: a small bite, a small stinging warning: this is the place of your people. But look how gently the wild grasses move in the air that stirs over the *graves, and look how the Queen Anne's lace reflects Celtic circles. Wheels within wheels, "way up in the middle of the air."*

• • •

W E had one week to travel around Ireland before returning to the convent in Sligo for the workshop. Going to the five-thousand-year-old passage grave at Newgrange was an important experience for me: the mystical spirals carved in the rock at the opening and deep in the tomb moved me, connected me to the solid rock of this planet, to the tremendous power of light and dark, to the imagining of people like myself in a time before this time, and to those who will follow after me in a time that is yet to be. Turning and turning, the spirals called to me as a sign of something spiritual that antedates our systematic theologies; an evidence of spirituality that cannot be reduced to explanation. I felt myself grateful that every theory had to be qualified as "simply a possibility." Something too old for us to call "God" or "Goddess" or any other name. But something holy. Clearly, something holy.

And after Moat, we visited other old Quaker graveyards. As the two weeks wore on, I began to think of those ancestors as persons, rather than as English. I began to think of them as Quakers, pacifists, plain dressed passionate people in flight from Anglicanism in England, aliens on Irish soil, soon to leave for America, still seeking religious freedom. I began to think kindly of them.

We returned to Sligo. On the first day back, while Máire was lost in the great main house of the convent, upstairs where the likes of me were not permitted to tread, and I was safely settled in the guest house out back, my kindness toward the old Quakers moved me to dig out Mama's book of genealogy and open it, and for the first time since I typed it for her many years before, actually *read* the thing.

The shock was stunning. In addition to the three or four names Mama thought were Irish, there was the main family line for which the book was named: Ridgway. And the patriarch of that family was "Richard Ridgway, the immigrant," who in the 1700s was given land in the "new world" by William Penn adjoining his own. Although the exact connection cannot be proven, Richard came from the neighborhood of, and spelled his name identically to, a man in England who could have been his grandfather or great uncle: Sir Thomas Ridgway. And Sir Thomas Ridgway was "treasurer at war" in Ireland. He was the man who recommended to the crown the destruction of the Irish Catholic clergy. He was one of the men at the heart of genocidal policies: intentional starvation, battering rams against the cottages of Irish Catholics. My mother's book quotes Sir Thomas Ridgway, writing to Sir Robert Cecil, the future Lord Salisbury, in 1603:

> Of late the country swarms with priests, Jesuits, seminaries, friars and Romanish bishops; if there be not speedy means to free this kingdom of this rabble, much mischief will burst forth in very short time. There are here so many of this wicked crew as are able to disquiet four of the greatest kingdoms in Christendom. It is high time they were banished, and none to receive or aid them.

What do we know, underneath what we think we do not know? Did I, at some subliminal level, remember what I had typed for Mama so many years ago? Is that why I didn't want to claim my English ancestors on Irish soil? Does the blood, do the very cells of our bodies hold the memories of our ancestors? Of "our people?" Can those whose genes we carry, those who have died, speak to us in dreams? Can they speak in some other knowing deeper than dreaming? Did my father's mother speak to me in a dream? Or is there a simpler explanation, did she tell me before my fourth year that she was part Indian? And did I unconsciously remember her words in my fifties, so it surfaced as a dream after the death of Mama, who had successfully kept my grandmother's memory repressed all those years? Did I just — as they said in the Missouri of my childhood — *clean forget* what was in Mama's book, and resist my English ancestors out of pure laziness? Or do the cells of my body hold written along the encoded pattern of my physical being, some memory of my father's mother and Mama's ancient grandfather?

It occurred to me not to tell Máire about Sir Thomas Ridgway. When I called home and told one of my daughters, her first words were, *"Whatever you do, don't tell Máire!"* I was afraid to tell her. She had worked so hard to reconnect me with "my people"; and my people include literally, actually, the very minister of war who was the exact and most cruel enemy of her people. I could hear her sweet voice singing the sorrowful songs of exile, recounting the terrible tales of genocide.

But of course I told her, immediately, when she came back to the guest house. To not do so would have made it impossible for me to lead the workshop. I could not ask of her, and of others, the radical openness that writing demands and withhold so important a secret. We sat in silence, the information between us, for quite a long time. And as much as my memory has retained of each visit to Ireland, I don't remember what was said between us that night. I think not very much. I know that I felt great sorrow, and distance open between us. Even in that sorrow and that distance, however, I felt that there was a radical importance to the bridge we were building across the forms our difference took: I was out of the church, she was a professional religious; I was Protestant, she was Catholic; I was possibly a descendant — surely a relative — of the specific English man who hurt her people, she was descended from Irish rebels who suffered jail for independence from England; I was a married wife and mother, she was a celibate nun.

That night, I am certain we both stood in the knowledge that none of us are free from the history that made us. When she went back into the convent I sat alone in the small, cinder block building that once had been music rooms for a huge convent school, but now served as bedrooms for guests of the few, mostly very elderly nuns who lived in the cavernous building, keeping the ancient traditions.

MÁIRE, WHO FEEDS THE WILD CAT?

Behind the convent a wild
cat is ill. She sleeps
in a fine mist of rain
on the warm hood
of a cooling automobile.
She's sick, poor thing,
you say. You say
she's too sick to run away.

And you are cloistered here
uneasy now in all the old
familiar habits, awkward
in the raw world, its own
severe conventions, language
of fashion, innuendoes. Rules.

From the window of the guest house
I study the convent walls,
the remote third floor
where no one may go but
nuns of your particular order.
The wall is fortress high

and fortress thick. Inside,
the Sisters smile, repeating
and repeating one another's names:
Rosario, Saint Ambrose, Immaculate.

Outside, where a mist of rain
has chilled the bone of this day,
a wild cat watches,
too sick to run away.

4

F O R years I have been working with images of my childhood — writing them into poems, slowly bringing into focus Mama, my father, my brother, and myself as a child. That process began after I went back to graduate school, in my forties, to get a master of fine arts degree in creative writing. Another poet in the program, whom I will call Naomi, read poems to me about her childhood and encouraged me to write from my own life experience. All that I was taught about writing to that point blocked the possibility of writing out of personal experience. To write autobiographically, I was taught, was "self indulgent" and "confessional." And those were pejorative terms.

But Naomi was passionately committed to searching for and writing out of her own personal truth, her own lived experience, and she wanted me to do the same. On one evening in particular she sat on my couch and told me stories about how she cared for her handicapped younger sister, how when she was a teenager she traveled back and forth across the state line between Georgia and Florida to attend an art school. When she went home that evening, I sat alone remembering our conversation. I saw Naomi in my mind at thirteen, on her way to art school. Something about being thirteen was crucial for me. I asked myself, "Where was I when I was thirteen?" The answer snapped into my mind like a whip: clear, exact, immediate: *Don't think about that. That will hurt Mama.*

I began again. Naomi, I said to myself, was taking art lessons when she was thirteen. Where was I? And again the answer, sharp, warning, *No! Don't think about that. That will hurt Mama.* My body felt it, as clear and stinging as a slap across the face.

Later I would remember how my mother had repeated hundreds of times, "Never, never tell anybody how we live. I would be so ashamed." But that night, all that was clear to me was the internal voice that was so instant with its command: *"NO!"*

I sat through the night, stunned by the power of the litany in my head. As the hours passed, the words of the litany changed gradually. I began to say, "Naomi had a childhood. Mama had a childhood. Where is my childhood?" And the answer: *No. That will hurt Mama.* Then it changed again: Mama had her childhood, and Mama has *my* childhood. I said that over and over, beginning to rock, as if I were a very small child, and finally there arose in me a huge "NO!" of my own. At five o'clock in the morning, gray light moving into the apple tree outside my window, I wrote the first words of truth about my childhood. It was a poem, addressed to Naomi. It began: *"There were maggots in the canned peas on the stove,/ and rats came up the furnace duct when I was a child . . ."*

One of the most dramatic things that happened as I began to write about my childhood grew out of a memory of my father. I had only three memories of him, each one like an old, still snapshot in my mind. The clearest was that he took me with him to the outhouse, and peed.

I had told Mama this memory, and she had reacted with disgust. "Isn't that awful! A grown man urinating in front of a little girl!"

I never had occasion to tell anyone else this memory, and each time I mentioned it to Mama I got the same response. I believed her interpretation when I was a child, and without even realizing they existed, I carried with me the assumptions embedded in her interpretation when I became a woman.

    Naomi and I were both in our forties, both had families, both had published poetry and other writing, and intended to teach writing when we finished our degrees. I was frustrated; the writing that I had been doing was primarily for the theater, and I wanted to write poems but was not satisfied with what was coming. Naomi was certain that I should try to write about my father. I told her I only had insignificant fragments of memories. Her tenacity was remarkable. She wanted me to look at one of the memories more closely. I resisted, saying, "Naomi, there's nothing there to write about. All I remember, I have told you."

    "Tell me again about the outhouse," she said.

    "He takes me to the outhouse, and he pees. That's it."

    "What do you see when he first takes you outside?"

    "The yard."

    "What about the yard?"

    "It was gravelly."

    "No grass?"

    "No grass."

    She waited, and in the silence I saw the yard, the fence, and I added, "It was a little place called Nixa — only they pronounced it "Nixie." Next door to the house there was a cheese factory on the other side of a chain-link fence. He worked there."

    "What happens when he takes you out of the house?"

    "Nothing, Naomi. We walk across the yard to the outhouse."

    "And then?"

    I think I laughed then. I laugh now, remembering her persistence. The image of a snapping turtle comes to mind — how they hang on to something once they have it in their mouths! "And then," I said, "we went into the outhouse and he peed!"

"Wait a minute," Naomi said. "You see more than that! What was the outhouse like?"

"It was just your usual outhouse . . . "

"What about the wood? Was it rough, or planed?"

And with that question, for the first time I began to take this seriously, because suddenly I realized that I *did* know — and see — more than I was saying. More, in fact, than I was allowing myself to see, or know. And so more humbly, I responded, "It's rough. Unplaned. Except for right around the holes — around the holes it's been sanded smooth."

"How many holes are there?"

"Two. A big one and a little one."

"What else do you see?"

"There are green flies."

"How do you feel about the flies?"

The first surprise. "I — uh — I don't know. I think I like them. They're pretty. Very green. I think it's a nice green — an intense green."

"What else?"

"There's a smell —"

"How do you feel about the smell?"

Second surprise. "Well, it's intense too — but I guess it's OK. Yeah, it's OK. I don't mind the smell."

"What else do you see?"

At this point I felt myself truly small in that little wooden outhouse. It seemed almost a physical act as I looked up and saw a bucket hanging on a nail. In the bottom of the bucket were holes — many holes, that had been punched out with a nail. I described it, and told Naomi, "I have no idea what that bucket is doing there, but I couldn't make up a thing like that!" Later I asked Mama if there was a bucket hanging on the wall of the outhouse where we lived in "Nixie."

"Yes," she said. "That's how we took a shower."

Even before I had this confirmation from Mama, I knew the bucket was real, and I was beginning to feel a kind of awe as I saw more than I ever dreamed I could see of myself at age four.

Naomi turned the questions toward my father. "What is he doing now?"

"He's unzipping his fly."

"And now?"

"He's pulling his penis out. He's peeing."

"Tell me what you see."

"I see a yellow arc of urine."

Her voice was very soft. "How do you feel about that?"

"I feel OK about it. He's not bothering me. He's just peeing, and it's very interesting. It's different from the way I pee." Suddenly my lifetime understanding of my father shifted. I liked being out in that outhouse with him. It was friendly. It was interesting. And besides, Mama was in the house crying, and he had taken me out of the house because he was protecting me — giving me a "break." I was as certain of that fact as I had been certain of the bucket with the nail holes. And I was certain that I wanted to be taken out of the house. My father — in that memory — was not a bad man at all! He was my friend, and I was happy to be with him. It is not too much to say that in that experience of looking closer and closer at a fragmentary memory, I was given back my lost father.

Countless times writers in my workshops have told me they have no memories of their childhood, or only very fragmentary, meaningless snippets of memories. What happened to me in dialogue with Naomi about this memory convinced me that every human being has gold in his or her hands in the tiniest fragment of a memory, but often has no idea of the treasure that such a fragment may hold.

In 1938, when Mama divorced my father, she tried farming at a Holiness community called Mount Zion for two years, then taught in a one-room country school for a year where we lived in a house trailer in the school yard, then moved Sam and me to Wichita, Kansas, where she worked for two years sharpening drill bits at Boeing Aircraft Company, making B29s for the second World War.

As the war in Europe wound down, Boeing began to lay off women working on war planes. Mama took us back to St. Louis and found work as a "practical nurse," sent out by an agency to private patients in need of all-night care. She had completed one year of nurse's training when she was young, and had worked as a midwife for a short time in the Ozark mountains. She liked nursing, but work was always temporary, and the places she found for us to live were temporary, too. She constantly searched for something better; we moved so many times during our childhood I transferred to different schools thirteen times in the first eight grades.

One of those transfers was soon after returning to St. Louis from Wichita. When I was eleven and Samuel was nine and a half, she put us into an orphanage and moved alone to 4039 Olive Street, third floor, rear. It was to that apartment that I returned a year and a half later, and there we stayed through my four years of high school.

Olive Street ran the length of the city, from the river out to the suburbs. We were forty blocks from the river in an area where two streetcar lines used one track and cheap stores, and pawn shops and taverns were crowded between the few old Victorian buildings that remained as tenements.

The most consistent, and perhaps the strongest image that emerged as I began to write about childhood was of myself at thirteen, newly home from the orphanage, sitting in the third story window in that house on Olive Street, looking down at streetcars passing at night. They rattled like tin cans full of light; they were taking women in fur coats to the opera. That's what I thought. Of course it was not so; the coats were fake fur, worn by waitresses on their way to night jobs, downtown. Women in fur coats did not ride the Delmar streetcar to the opera. But I believed they did, and I believed they looked out their streetcar windows and saw only their own reflections. They did not look up to the third floor window of the gray building on Olive Street. They did not see me. They did not know there was a thirteen-year-old girl in the window wanting to go to the opera. I *willed* them to look up. I *willed* them to see. And knowing they did not, I hated them with a pure and perfect hatred. I looked across store roofs to the dome of the St. Louis Cathedral, which I believed was plated with gold. It caught the light of the setting sun even after darkness filled the canyon of the street below me. I sat in the window and repeated and repeated a vow: *I will get out of here. Someday, I will get out of here. I will get out and I will go to the opera. But I will never, never forget.*

For a long time I believed that it was the house itself, the ugliness of the apartment, the dirt, the lack of closets, the close space, that was traumatic. After years of writing poems and journal entries about my childhood, however, I came to understand that what was traumatic was *coming home from the orphanage.* Before I went to the orphanage, I did not see how we lived. But when I came home, I had to try *not* to see. That was traumatic.

• • •

The bed. Mama says it's a "Hollywood bed." That means it's a little wider than a twin bed, but not as wide as a full bed. It stands in a little alcove place in one of the two rooms we live in on Olive Street. Mama, Sam, and me. Mama hung a sheet on a rope in front of the bed, but we never close the sheet. There's no window in the alcove. The rope sags, the sheet has gotten limp and dirty. There's no closet in our apartment. There are books and trash and food wrappers piled at both ends of the bed and in the corners of the alcove where the sheet hangs — there's junk there piled as high as the bed. There's a table, two straight-backed chairs and a studio couch in the room. They've got junk on them, too. The table is piled with dirty dishes and papers and moldy food crusted in aluminum pans and maybe clothes and maybe anything. The other room is a little kitchen. A rattletrap metal sink hangs loose from the wall and bare pipes come up from the floor behind it. On the stove another pan holds canned peas; lots of times white maggots squirm slowly among the peas. It's hot in St. Louis, and there are no screens on the windows. At night a rat comes up through the broken grate over the furnace duct, if the brick gets moved off it. In and out of everything, thousands of roaches move, and hide.

The bed. It's hot and sweaty. It has roaches in it. It's not my bed. Mama sleeps there all day when she has a job, and at night when she doesn't. Sam sleeps on the couch when he's home. Mostly he's at foster homes. Once Mama wanted to get a better home for Sam and she called a social service agency. They came unexpectedly to do a "home study." Mama demanded to read the report. It said someone in that family doesn't have a bed. It said maybe my brother was sleeping with Mama. She cried and showed me the report. "It's not true! It's not true!" she said. I wrapped my arms around her. I comforted her. I said "Of course not! Of course it's not true!"

The bed. Mama's body, sweaty, next to mine. My own breath—no breath—no air to breathe—roaches. Mama's sweaty body on the dirty sheets. A narrow bed. She wants my arms around her. "I need you," she says. "I need you to hold me while I fall asleep." She pulls me to her. "We used to call this 'spooning,'" she says. "Hold me and pull your knees up behind my knees," she says. "There, sleep like that." She sleeps. I am wide awake. I am thirteen. I can't breathe. The air of the two rooms is heavy hot. I am ashamed that I don't want to hold Mama. Poor Mama. She can't cope. I should be happy to be home from the orphanage. Poor Mama. Tomorrow I will stay home from school and clean the house. I'll clean it all, and I'll really really try not to be mad when she throws things down on the floor.

• • •

I was forty-two-years old when I turned around in my mind for the first time and asked *who* in that family did not have a bed.

No one raped me there. My mother did not intend harm. She was lonely, and emotionally needy. In many ways the pattern was familiar — she acting the role of child, and I acting the role of comforter, reassurer, parent. But I was a child, and exactly at the point where I should have been establishing my own independence, my own adolescent sexual identity, Mama was — with a terrible innocence — consuming me.

I have no memory of going to sleep as a child, except at the orphanage, and twice when I slept in other people's houses — Aunt Nellie's, a cousin's — and then the memories are crystalline, glorious: the clean rooms, the things on dressers in casual but uncluttered ease, the window curtains, the pictures on the walls, the made beds, the bare floor in one, the soft rug in the other, the absence of roaches and rats, the slow, gentle drift into sleep. Those two memories are so clear and special, looking at them, writing about them helped me to see almost as a negative image what the rest of my nights were like, and what the orphanage meant to me.

5

THE orphanage wasn't bad. Edgewood Children's Home was in Webster Groves, a wealthy suburb of St. Louis. It was lonely after they wouldn't let my brother stay, after he was sent to a foster home. But other than being lonely, it wasn't bad. There was a quietness there, an order, that I had never experienced. The quietness of physical objects in place, of events on schedule, of responsibilities assigned and kept. There was the smell of lemon furniture oil, the feeling of the cloth in my hands, myself on my knees polishing the steps in the wide, sunny front hall of the girl's dormitory. There was learning that a staircase can be polished.

The staircase I came home to on Olive Street smelled bad. The one bathtub for the eight families in the building held a constant yellow pool that smelled like urine. The bathroom was utterly untended. I peed squatting, one foot balanced on either edge of the ancient toilet bowl, holding my clothes carefully so nothing but the soles of my shoes would touch my surroundings. We stood in line in the dark hallway — men, women, children from other apartments, the "manager," an aging wino who held a milk bottle full of yellow pee in his hand, and me—waiting our turn, never speaking, shame as thick as the heavy air. It never occurred to me to clean the bathroom. I was a child. As dirty, as shameful as it was, nevertheless I fantasized making it into my room. I could sleep in

Wake Up Laughing

the bathtub, I thought. It was the only place where I locked a door and was in a space no one else could enter.

At the orphanage, everyone had a bed of her own. I didn't mind being lined up with several other little girls in a big room, each of us with one bed and one dresser. I couldn't remember ever having had a bed of my own; I always slept with Mama. She didn't often wash sheets. She never made up the bed. Here all the beds were made up, and smooth, and the sheets were clean. Everyone had her own chore to do; it felt like a privilege. As I worked, light from the front door fell on the clean wood I was polishing, and somewhere in another part of the building other girls were doing other chores, their voices mixed with the sound of a radio playing Frankie Layne, "The Cry of the Wild Goose."

Once a young social worker took me home with her for a weekend. She was not much more than college-age, pretty, with short dark hair and eyes that were kind. She was being kind. I knew she was being kind. In her bedroom I saw for the first time my whole body at once. I did not know anyone had a mirror long enough to see her whole self, and I said so, probably with considerable awe in my voice. She was pleased. "Then you just look as much as you want," she said, and left me alone in her bedroom.

Then she took me to lunch in a small restaurant downtown, near Famous Barr. There were two huge department stores in downtown St. Louis in those days. The restaurant was near them. On one side of the street was Famous Barr, on the other, a store that even then struck me as amazingly named: Hellrung and Grimm.

The restaurant was small, and crowded. Tables with white tablecloths were close together, and waiters in dark suits moved elegantly between them. We were seated at a small table in the center of the floor. The young social worker smiled at me, helped me to order from the large, glossy menu, and leaned back in her chair, smiling. We had nothing to talk about; I was eleven, she was probably twenty-two. What do you ask a kid who lives in an orphanage? "Tell me about your mother . . ." No. "Do you have a father at home . . ." No. Better not to mention home. We had covered sixth grade, did I like the teacher; and church, did I like the church; and the other kids in the orphanage, did I like them. I wasn't much help — what do you say to a social worker who is twice your age and being kind?

In the silence I took a reading on my situation. A white tablecloth. I could not remember ever in my life eating at a table with a tablecloth on it except maybe once when I was very young at Christmas at an aunt's house. At home we ate standing up, walking around, sitting on the edge of a chair with the junk on it pushed to one side. There was usually a slice of bologna between two slices of puffy white Wonder Bread. There was canned tomato soup. Packaged cookies. Everything came from Krogers, everything purchased ready to eat. We had no refrigerator, and the ice box usually had no ice in it. So we opened cans, or ate what we had brought home from Krogers that day. I remember being on my knees at one of the windows, praying with all my might to find ten cents somewhere on the floor, behind a chair, under a pile of dirty clothes. Ten cents would buy a loaf of bread.

The dirt, and the heat, and the discouragement. Mama told me the reason she put us in the orphanage was so we would learn good manners at the table. She wanted us, she said, to "get out of here." She said if we were going to get out of being poor, we would need good manners. She also said she couldn't cope, but I tried to not think about that. I just thought about the manners.

There was a white tablecloth on the table in the little restaurant. And silverware. It seemed to me that it was real silver — the beautiful, dull glow, the delicate pattern on the handles. A knife. Two forks. Two spoons.

Wake Up Laughing

The social worker saw me looking and explained about salad forks and dessert spoons. She told me not to worry; she would help me.

Then the food arrived. Thinking that there was one thing I did know, I slipped the napkin out from under its load of forks and opened it. It felt heavy, significant, big. Never before in my life had I been given a cloth napkin. I thought, *Oh, rich people eat like this! Educated people eat like this! I am here. It is now. Oh, perfect. I will make it.* It was the first experience in my life of feeling I had crossed over. I felt the belief: *I will get out of the shame. I am out. I am here.* I tucked a corner of the napkin into the neck of my blouse, and smoothed it down over my chest.

The young social worker in a flash reached across the table and pulled the napkin down, and there it was: that terrible instant when she was not smiling, when she was glancing to each side to see who might be watching. It was only an instant, and then she was smiling at me again, but the instant lasted forever. I failed the test. I failed to "pass." Who I really was had been revealed. The shame of the dirt at home, the maggots in the canned peas on the stove, everything was known, seen. I felt as if I would die until she delivered me, hours later, into the orphanage where I knew now I did not belong; it was too clean — where I did not belong, it was too orderly — where I was an impostor and a foreigner, but at least if I could be quiet enough, and good enough, I could survive until I could go home to Sarah and Olive Streets, where I did belong.

And I did go back to Mama. My brother Sam, whom I adored, never lived at home again.

BROTHER

> Your face in the dirty kitchen
> in the awful afternoon
> three stories up from the clanging street

trolleys and paper boys, winos and whores
Your face in the steamy air
of a St. Louis summer
on the top floor of a tenement
with no air
Your face   face to face
with a cop   his neat blue uniform
his billy stick   his round face
his fat hand holding his hat   his voice
Your face
his words   *some boys say*
you took a burning stick
and poked out a cat's eyes
is that true
Your face
is that true
is that true
hot air unmoving in the hot room
no one moving in the hot room
it's fifty years later and no one has moved
in the hot room on the third floor
forever and forever your face
your eyes   your voice   your one word:
No.

In middle age, when I began writing about my childhood, it was always images of that house. Sometimes it seemed I would never work my way through to another emotional landscape. I dreamed that house so often that finally I went for eight sessions with a therapist who specialized in Jungian interpretation of dreams. When I asked, "Won't I ever the hell be free of that place?" she answered, "You dream of it so often because you left a part of yourself back there, and that part of you feels abandoned." And what if every motion we ever made goes on and on, like a ripple in the air, like a radio wave, like a memory that we can't shake, like a relationship we need to lay down and cannot. We are not only who we are here and now. We are also all of the parts of ourselves that we may think we have left behind.

And so I flew back to Missouri, and I took all the parts of myself with me, whether I wanted to or not.

6

I AM flying to Missouri to find Leona. To find my lost father, and his lost people. It is August after my June workshop in Ireland. I have been in California leading workshops and will stop in St. Louis on my way home and spend several days in Missouri.

When the flight sets down in St. Louis, I rent a car, and before driving into the hills of southern Missouri to find her, I return to Olive Street.

The violin shop, of course, is gone. It stood in the middle of the block, across the streetcar tracks. It was a quiet, dark window between tawdry shops. The window glass was a big square with gold letters painted in an arc: VIOLINS. Inside, on a window shelf, the mysterious shapes of violins, cellos: the deep golden rosy wood, the silence of the shapes, the silent possibility of symphony. There was a wanting in me so strong it felt like a treasure. Wanting that quiet, that deep richness, that inevitable music under the clamor of the streetcar behind me, under the shout of the middle-aged paper boy on the corner of Sarah and Olive. The shape of silence was the shape of music. There will never be a symphony equal to the one that lay hidden in the silence of the curved side of that cello standing behind the violin that lay flat on the dusky window shelf, an opening into another world, crowded between the beauty salon on one side, where women sat attached to curlers, each curler attached to a cord, each cord attached to a huge metal cap — and the dingy store that sold washing machines on the other side.

The violin shop is gone. And the beauty salon, and the appliance store, and the tavern. On my side of Olive Street, the several taverns, the pawn shop, the abandoned donut shop, its cracked window glass, its faded poster with the words — *As you travel on through life, brother/ Whatever be your goal/ Keep your eye upon the donut/ And not upon the hole!* — gone. The Congress moving picture show and the house where I once lived are gone. The entire block on my side of the street has been leveled. Even the rubble has been carted away. Up near Sarah Street some rebuilding has begun — a row of tidy townhouses, apartments or condos, built back along short walks from the spine of sidewalk that runs as it always has beside the street. The streetcars are gone, the tracks removed, even the asphalt that covered them is old now. The street is smaller, more narrow than I remembered.

Where 4039 once stood, the city is opened as a mouth might be opened, the building vanished as a tooth might be extracted, the exquisite pain gone, the odor of sickness removed, the raw wound healing now — tender, but healing. Where there once was a row of tenements, there is now: air. Air! Space, and air.

The city is opened and it stands open. All the way to Vandeventer Street, a long block, empty. A whole field laid open to sunlight in the middle of an old, cranky city. The houses gone. The sky above seems surprised, revealed: blue. And over the ground where for generations heavy three-story houses sat, false-fronted Victorian ladies in a row, ugly, hiding their dirty memories, their miserable repressions, now there has arisen a field of cornflowers. The blossoms are a shock of blue — a blue that will not allow itself to survive if placed in a vase; a blue that, when picked, drains immediately, vanishes, leaving you with a stained weed and the sense that you have exceeded your right on earth, committed a violence against blue, so that you throw it away with a touch of shame and a twist of recognition.

The sidewalk along the edge of the field has crumbled, has lost the battle with tough prairie grass, a battle it was waging when I was a child. At last the grass has won — the sidewalk is a ruin. Roller-skating there, even though it made the skating difficult, I had rejoiced for every blade of tough grass pushing against a crack, every victory of the prairie. I skated at thirteen remembering the creek bed at Mt. Zion in southern Missouri where I had waded when I was five. I skated remembering the fossils in a deep cut in an old road near Fort Leonard Wood beyond Aunt Nellie's filling station where I went alone when I was ten. I imagined fossils hidden deep beneath the asphalt and the concrete of Olive Street. I reached down to them, and loved them. My mother said my father's people were no good. She spoke of her people as *her* people. And so I claimed fossils as my only ancestors. I knew who I was; I belonged to the rock.

Standing on the ruined sidewalk in my middle age, looking at the field clean of houses, seeing how the wild grass hurries to come back, an arc of happiness joined me to the child I used to be. I have kept the promise she made to herself: I did get out. I wanted to reach out and touch her, incorporeal there in the air. I wanted to take her with me to the "opera" — to the prèmiere of my libretto in Carnegie Hall. I wanted to take her by the hand and show her the work I do without pay and without a sponsoring organization in public housing projects in New England. I wanted her to see me *seeing* a child in a housing project window. I wanted her to know that I hadn't forgotten.

HAD I waited another year to return to St. Louis, the field would likely have been filled with new houses. The cornflowers would have been gone to mowed grass and marigolds. The ancient remnant of sidewalk

Wake Up Laughing

would have been gravel, lost under a new concrete walk. I stood looking at the empty lot. The ghost of the house floated, almost substantial. Under it and through it, moving ever so slightly in the Mississippi River valley air, were hundreds and hundreds of blue cornflowers.

Near the sidewalk , hidden in tough grass, there was one small cluster of stones. I found a single gray slate from the false front of the house, and in the weeds, sitting as if offered to me on a table, a heavy white coffee mug full of packed, gravelly earth. I stuck the stem of one cornflower into the mug, knowing that I would hold the blue in my mind after it drained away. Then I picked up the mug, still filled with soil, and the slate, put them in my rented car, and drove up Olive Street to Spring, one block on Spring to Grandell Square, and parked beside the church that paid my way through college.

7

THE church is a shell. Time past and time present collide; I am in two times simultaneously — I am a kid walking alone up the steps to church, its white stone bell tower, carved stone capitals on the front porch columns, stone leaves of ferns. So much of the history of this city, named for a French saint, is held in the silent language of this old building: the ferns are *fleur-de-lis*, symbols of French Monarchy, the square, sensible architecture was designed for Union soldiers in the Civil War, the church named to welcome them: "Union Methodist." Gone. The huge stained-glass window, organ music. The robed choir processing toward the altar down the middle aisle, their hymnals open to page number one, their voices: *Holy, Holy, Holy, Lord God Almighty/ Early in the morning, our song shall rise to Thee . . .* " I hear it as if I were that kid, walking up the steps. And as if in double-exposure, I am also a woman with gray hair looking at a stone shell, the rooms inside demolished, workmen's drills whining like insects through the arched openings that had been windows.

A peeling, uneven, hand-lettered sign hangs over the great wooden doors: APOSTOLIC FAITH. And in smaller print: *Pastor* . . . and a man's name. *Black*, I think. The last congregation was black. If they were poor white, the sign might read something like "FULL BIBLE PENTECOSTAL CHURCH OF GOD." I imagine black gospel singing, the choir members,

Wake Up Laughing

their robes, their motion in the sanctuary. And now those voices, those stories, too, vanished. Layers of history.

I walk up onto the stone porch, past a smaller sign: HARD HATS REQUIRED, and look through the open doors. A cave. A huge, open space. Dirt at the bottom. A bare, incongruous light bulb hanging in open space at the end of a long extension cord, its light inconsequential in the vast gloom. And the sounds of men working, calling to each other beyond a wooden scaffolding.

They aren't going to tear it down, I think. *They would have blasted it, or swung a ball against it. They are going to keep the white stone tower, the arched windows, the columns. But it won't be a church, ever again.* I step down from the porch, look up. Grand Avenue. The great old theaters still stand where they stood in the fifties: the Fox, the Shubert. Heart of the theater district. Urban renewal.

I turn back to the church. *Ghost*, I say to the stone walls, the square bell tower. *Ghost.*

This church was the door I walked through to get out of poverty. It was not a door that was open to everyone. The church like the society in which it existed, was classist. I went to them; they did not come to me. I did not look like them.

One day, I couldn't find anything to wear to school. Everything was dirty, crumpled into corners on the floor, and I had grown enough that almost nothing fit me any more. My body shape was changing. The old clothes didn't fit over my new breasts. There was nothing to wear to school, but staying home in two dirty rooms all day was unthinkable. Mama was sleeping there because she worked at night. I tried to think of a story that would fit my wearing one of Mama's nurses uniforms; I couldn't think of anything. Finally I put on a satin formal that she had bought from a Salvation Army store to cut up for little cushions someday if we ever got a couch. It was low cut, plum color, and had a bustle in the back. I thought I'd just pretend that I was going someplace special right after school, and if anybody asked, that's what I'd say. I wore some of her high-heeled shoes with it, but they hurt my feet and so I put them in my locker and put on my gym shoes, cloth sneakers. I walked through the halls of the high school with my back straight, looking straight ahead, pretending I had good reason to look the way I looked. But Miss Warner, my English teacher noticed. She asked me to stay after class, and said, "Honey, don't you have anything better to wear?"

The church helped me; I walked in their door, and they saw me. They did not see, they did not try to help my brother.

The church was racist. Once I brought with me to church a girl named Charlotte whom my mother called "a mulatto." Charlotte lived downstairs from us, with her white grandmother. Often I heard the old woman screaming, "Nigger! nigger!" — the sound coming up the furnace duct into our apartment. I was told by the pastor never to bring Charlotte again because he was trying to get the church to put me through college, and if she came with me they might not do it. Charlotte and I were both sixteen. I was desperate to get out of the trap I was caught in, and I believed college was the only way out, but I felt sick in response to the warning. I agonized; I prayed; I decided to take her anyway. The following week I asked her to go with me, but her grandmother said she could never go again. She was Catholic. To go to a Protestant church was sin.

The church was sexist. God was "He," and I sang along with no consciousness of the implications, sang my heart out to the glory of the "Fatherhood of God" and the "Brotherhood of Man."

It was a church left over from the days when my neighborhood had been more genteel. In my sophomore year at college the congregation moved to a nicer neighborhood in the suburbs. That same year, the quiet man who was our pastor, Gerald Harris, and his wife were killed when their car was struck by a train. I never attended the new church, but the congregation that had moved did not abandon me; they continued to send money to college for me until I graduated, and as I write these words forty years later, tears of gratitude for their kindness and frustration for their blindness, rise.

SOMEONE, years later, said to me, "Don't you see? You were just their 'token poor person.'" I was furious. It was true that they were racist, sexist, classist. It was true that they never looked twice at my brother, whose need was equal to mine, but who did not make good grades, teach in their Sunday school, meet their criteria. Nevertheless, Gerald Harris, whatever his failings, whatever the failings of the congregation he served, did *see me*. Because of him, somebody paid my way to college. Somebody got me out, saved my life, set me free.

And I am not a "token." I am a country all to myself, a continent, a world. I stand before the broken shell of a church, and I overflow with love. *Amazing grace, how sweet the sound/that saved a wretch like me.* I have heard people complain about the archaic sensibility of the word "wretch." John Newton, who wrote those words, was a reformed slave trader. He said "wretch" because he knew what it meant to be "wretched." I know what it is to be free, because I know what it is to be in bondage. No matter how inadequate the people of that church were, this one thing they did: they set me free.

8

It is imperative to remember the moment when your little brother stood before you at the hot-dog stand. But why that moment and not another? Why not one of the multitude of moments that are lost? Remember the sunlight on the hot sidewalk. Remember the sticky sweat, the cotton of the long ago, pink-print, feed-sack, little-girl dress.

Remember the long hill at the Art Museum. Remember going there alone with your brother. Remember the sidewalk, the metal roller skates, the skate key on a shoestring around your neck. Remember how you started down the hill, how the wind was in your face, how you knew your brother was watching, how the green grass of the hill was tilting, and the trees were rushing by and the pond was far, far below, at the bottom of the hill, and at the top, behind you, the art museum with huge Saint Louis riding nowhere on his horse, and the carved lions on either side of the steps and inside — inside — the mummy and the huge middle-aged woman, the words there beneath her naked body: MIDDLE AGED WOMAN. Her breasts, her buttocks, her belly, how it was round and no girdle made of Playtex and no sweat and middle-aged and not pretty but alright, alright to look that way, round belly and breasts that half hung down and thick thighs and no girdle just bronze and forever and forever and strong. And best of all the Egyptian cat, the holy, the divine, the worshipped, the perfect Egyptian cat, how its back curved like music, how beautiful that line was from

Wake Up Laughing

the head down the back, how that one line held everything together, everything, and the world made sense, and something was holy, holy, and it was bigger than the church, and the dirt and the hurt at home didn't matter, wouldn't last — what would last was what had already lasted, was bronze, was forever, a line, a curve down the back of a cat on a pedestal in the middle of a still room in the art museum and how the trees are going by too fast and the grass is coming up and the sidewalk isn't perfectly smooth and you're going to fall you've got to fall sooner or later you've got to fall now now let it be now and you turn off the sidewalk onto the grass you choose the fall and the world curves up to catch you in its green green arms and you fall and your brother comes running and he cries out are you OK — are you OK? *and you say,* yeah, yeah, I'm OK.

9

I HAVE one brother. No sister. One brother. I have tried many times to write this story. I gag, I falter, I digress. I have decided that gagging, faltering and digressing is the true form for this story. It is about what happened to Sam, but it is also about what happened to me *because of* what happened to Sam. Stories have a ripple effect. Once I read in a magazine about something called "the butterfly effect." In the tropics, a butterfly moves its great, delicate wings, and slightly stirs the atmosphere. That slight stir moves a leaf, which moves a twig, and the movement grows until there is a hurricane off the coast of Florida.

If I were to write this story calmly, without digressing, it would not be true.

Sam was kicked out of the orphanage at age nine.

ONCE I went into an empty apartment with a friend who was considering a divorce. It was summer. Late summer. August perhaps. The room was hot, still. Intense sun through high uncurtained Victorian windows warmed old, wooden floorboards. My friend lingered in the kitchen, worried about the ancient appliances. I went into the front room alone. There on the floor were a dozen dead bumblebees — their bodies little fuzzy puffs; their legs and wings intact. In the hot sun I had a sense of their buzzing, their intense little summer-long lives, their entrapment there in that vast tomb, their death.

Today, as I try to write about my brother, the image of the bees keeps getting caught in it, tangled in it. Something lost, something preserved, something very beautiful, something . . .

When I was a child, I had a constant companion.

Bumblebees still as death in the shells of their bodies. In the quiet room, the buzz of their histories.

• • •

FACTS

1. Mama puts us in an orphanage. I am eleven. Samuel is nine.

2. He is sent home from the orphanage after three months. Mama tells me the director said he did something sexual. I ask Mama, "Did he?" She answers, "I don't know." I try and try to think what a nine-year-old might do that is sexual, that is so bad. Fifty years later he says older boys stole his pants, and he ran naked after them. When they were caught, the boys blamed him.

3. He is sent to a series of foster homes and orphanages. He never lives at home again.

4. At seventeen, he is in a Presbyterian orphanage. The head of it says they can't keep him any more. Says he should go into the army; it will "make him or break him." Tells Mama to sign the paper. She signs. He enters the United States army on his seventeenth birthday.

5. Repeatedly he is late returning from leave. Later he says he was an alcoholic when he took his first drink at age seventeen.

6. Remains in army for two years, stationed at Fort Bragg, North Carolina, and then at Barstow, California.

7. Goes on leave. Is late getting back to base. Put in stockade on desert in Southern California. He is nineteen years old.

8. Guard tells Sam and another soldier in the stockade, a twenty-one-year-old, to sit outside the stockade on a bench in the shade of the building. The older boy says to Sam, "Let's take that jeep and leave." They do so, parking the jeep on camp property near the highway.

9. Hitchhikes north to San Francisco. Declared AWOL by the Army.

10. My mother is notified that if he is not back by a certain date he will be considered "a deserter."

I WAS in college at Fayette, Missouri. My mother was working nights in St. Louis. When she got the word from the army that Sam was missing and would be considered a deserter, she called me at the college and told me to quit school and go with her to California. It was the second half of my senior year. I told my professors I had to go. They called me to a meeting in a classroom. There were two of them, Dr. Perry, English; Dr. Hicks, Philosophy. They told me bluntly that I was a poor girl on a full scholarship and if I left I would never get back in, and my family's problems would still be there waiting for me in four more months after I graduated. "You can help your family far more by finishing school," Dr. Perry said. "You won't help them by destroying yourself. Don't be a fool."

I had never "disobeyed" Mama. I had been so unnaturally "good," it was sick. I had never smoked a cigarette; never tasted beer or wine; I was a fundamentalist Christian who had always done exactly what I was told to do. Now, for the first time in my life, I told Mama "NO." Her life was out of control. She was living in a pit; clothes, magazines, junk covered the floor. Dirt. She was depressed and angry. She needed my brother's crisis to break apart the intolerable world she had created for herself. She raged; she cried; she accused me of being selfish and ambitious. *"You would walk over your own family to get to the top,"* she said over and over again. *"You don't love us. You don't love us. Alright, go on. Be selfish, you little whore. We'll get along just fine without you."*

I DID stay to finish my senior year. My mother went to San Francisco, talked to people in the poorest sections of the city, was befriended by somebody on a falling-down houseboat. She did not find Sam. Two days before he would have been considered a deserter, he turned himself in and was scheduled for a court martial.

My mother asked to talk to an army chaplain. "Don't go to the court martial," he advised her. "Don't go. It will just upset you. He's only nineteen years old. He should never have been in the army. He's not army material. He has no criminal record; the worst that can happen is a bad conduct discharge, and he'll be out of the army with some of his veteran's benefits still applying. I'll be there; there's no reason for you to be there. Don't go."

She didn't go. I was still in school. Sam stood court martial by himself. Later, the chaplain said he was sorry. It didn't turn out as he expected.

THE older boy, who did have a criminal record — he had stolen guns from the base at Barstow and had sold them — that boy's father was a career military man. And so they gave to him for his defense the officer who usually was the prosecuting attorney, and Sam was made responsible for everything. At age nineteen, he was sentenced to a year in Lompoc Maximum Security Prison on the desert in Southern California, and given a dishonorable discharge. It was 1956; a dishonorable discharge was a kind of death sentence. Death to jobs, death to self-esteem. The twenty-one-year-old was given six months in a stockade and a bad conduct discharge.

WHEN I graduated from college I went immediately to California. My mother was living in a two-room apartment, her boxes still unpacked, spilling out onto the floor. She had never gone to see Sam. She said it would hurt her too much to see him like that. I went alone.

THE image has become stark, simple in my mind. Lompoc Maximum Security Prison. A high tower. Another high tower. A chain-link fence, high. Very high. In each tower, a man with a rifle in his hands paces, turns, paces, turns. This is not science fiction. I am here. I am twenty-two years old. My brother is not quite twenty-one. He has been here for months. He is behind the fence, under the gun, inside the stone wall. The man with the gun paces. Paces. He turns. Slowly. He is shadowed by a roof over the gun tower. Farther away along the outer wall I see other towers. Other little stick-figure men turning.

WERE there other people with me? Other women? Did we ride together on a bus out to the prison? All of us related to men who were too poor to buy their way out, too ignorant to know how to work the system as the other boy's father had worked it? Were there other women with me? Other women related to men who were "not army material?" All of us silent, miserable, sharing each other's secret? I don't remember other women. I remember aloneness as if there was nothing but the desert, blistered with gray buildings, gray stone walls on which little men with death in their hands turned. I remember the wall, the sun, the heat, the hurt, the men. The men, turning. Slowly.

I remember a room as if after long hallways. I remember being asked for his name. I remember not wanting to give it, as if the soldier who asked it were a green toad asking me for my treasure, the name of my brother, my only brother, my fair little boy in second grade whom I protected from the big kids in fourth grade: *"Don't you ever try to beat up on my brother!*

Don't you ever try! You'll have to beat me up, too, and don't you forget it, either!"

The green toad asked me twice and I knew it was the price I would have to pay. *Samuel,* I said. *Samuel.* I didn't say it means *"Asked of God."* I didn't say, either, that he was not "asked of God" — our mother already convinced that her marriage had been a mistake, me two and a half years old and no meat, no milk in that depression year except what she had in her breasts, so Sam's adult rib-cage shows signs of rickets. Mine, too, but it was 1936, the country was in trouble, and trouble always settles into the pockets of the poor.

Samuel, I said.

THE green toad told me to wait where I was. There were a dozen ugly couches, ugly wooden chairs in a bare room with several small openings in a wall, bars on the openings, men behind the bars, their faces intersected by metal, and women leaning their faces onto the bars, their hands through the bars, leaning.

THEY brought him to me. He was thin. He was nervous. We sat on a couch, side by side. *"You shouldn't have come here, Pat,"* he said. *"I didn't want you to see me here,"* he said. I said, *"love."* I said, *"love and love and love."* He said, *"I wouldn't tell you what goes on here for anything in the world."* His hair was yellow. He was still a boy.

IN my middle age, I go to an empty apartment with a friend. On the floor, in the hot sun, a dozen bumblebees lie dead. Their little bodies striped black and gold, their lives, their quick, beautiful lives. The intense sun, through the great, closed windows of the empty room.

10

SAM is a big man now: work shirt, suspenders, mustache; the kind of man you recognize, knowing instantly that he will make you laugh. He's a truck driver. He says he owes his life to Alcoholics Anonymous. His home, with his wife, Eve, is a refuge for kids in trouble: state kids, runaways, teenage mothers, retarded adults. Always the coffee pot is on; always it is full. And he is full of stories, as he almost always has been. He was my first love.

For years, after getting out of the army, he wandered through the South, doing day jobs, lost in alcoholism. During that time he appeared, once, at my door in New England. He had no suitcase; I knew what that meant: he had no home. He gave me a scrap of paper, folded and dirty, with a paragraph written on it in handwriting that I still believe only I could read. It was about motorcyclists from hell. It was vivid, powerful writing. I felt the demons that pursued him; I saw the vision that he wanted me to see. This is wonderful writing, I thought. He is an artist. But no one will ever know, because he doesn't know how to spell, how to type. He doesn't have the "manners" Mama put us in the orphanage to learn. He doesn't know what I learned somehow, somewhere: how to climb the ladder of the academic world.

He brought me another scrap of paper. A letter, he said, from my

Wake Up Laughing

father. Sam had been to Waynesville, Missouri, and had visited his father. My father. I was in my early thirties, three babies to care for. I had not yet questioned my mother's interpretation of my father.

Sam handed me a piece of paper. I unfolded it. It was the kind of cheap tablet paper with extra wide lines that young children use to learn to write. The words were in pencil. *"Dear Patsy,"* it said. *"I am so happy to hear that you are ready to acknowledge me as your daddy. Sam came to visit me. Please write to me. Love, Daddy."*

I might have been able to hear his meaning more clearly if he had not unwittingly reinforced my mother's lifelong message, *"He has another little girl now. He doesn't love you."* He included in his letter to me three small school pictures of his other children.

When Sam left, I tore the letter up and threw it away.

11

Five miles. Hot sun. Leaf shadow. I am down. Down low. Lower than the fence post. Watch the gravel road. Bare feet. Flint. Calcite crystal. Watch out! OW! Keep to the scrub grass at the side, or the little line of grass in the middle, or the hot, packed tire trails. Keep off the gravel. OW! Watch out! Buzz of grasshoppers. Ah! Turn off the road, take the little grassy trail through the field. Ah! Easy, easy on the summer feet. Run! Past the abandoned canning factory off to the right. Past the field of something growing in straight rows to the left. Run! Hot sun! Little flurries of alarmed grasshoppers rise from every footfall and I like it. I like them. Something rises inside me like a puff of happiness. Run!

Stop. The tree line that edges the creek. Stop. Breathe. Wait.

You are five years old and this is yours. This is your holy place. This is your private place. Wait until the breathing slows.

Quiet, now. Very quiet. Slow. Open the door, the space between the trees. Go in. There. Close the door behind you. There.

Now you are invisible.

Now you are the child of the crawdad. Now you are the child of the stones. Now you are the child of the silence. Now you are alone. No one can hurt you here. No one can ever go away. No one can see you here except the crawdad, and the crawdad doesn't go away. You will learn how to swim backwards into dark caves in the rock. You will learn to look out of the dark caves with your crawdad eyes; your body will be hidden, safe in the rock. But you will watch. You will see a little girl — her dress is pink and flowered. It is made out of a feed sack. There is red rickrack on the collar. She squats at the edge of the water and you look at her and she looks at you and the world is a green room. Its walls are trees, its floor is stone, and this moment is the secret of the woman who waits inside the child.

12

I AM closing in on my father's people. I am coming closer. I drive southwest from St. Louis, past Waynesville where Leona lives, to Douglas County in the Ozarks where I was born.

When I first became myself, conscious of myself as a person alone and distinct in the world, I was a five-year-old child playing alone in a creek bed, deep in rural Missouri. Mama was a young woman then. She had left the man who fathered her two children (his curly hair, his country music, his whoring and drinking and repeated repentance), and returned to the Holiness school on a hill called Mount Zion, five miles outside of Ava, where I was born. Holiness people are radical in their fundamentalism. She could no longer be contained by their discipline, but neither was she convinced by her father's complete rejection of all Christian doctrine. I remember her crying on her knees once at the altar as a kind lady led me outside to play in the shade of an oak tree. There was a delicate sensitive plant there, and I thought about my mother inside crying as I touched the tiny leaves gently and watched them slowly close. Whatever that moment at the altar was about, it did not happen again. It is the only memory I have of my mother in a church.

Wake Up Laughing

She moved us into an old farmhouse on the school property. I was happy there — the great hickory trees, the cow and goat, the tabernacle across a dirt road where I heard singing in the long, summer evenings —

> *I'm livin' on the mountain,*
> *Underneath a cloudless sky, praise God!*
> *I'm drinkin' at the fountain,*
> *That never shall run dry,*
> *Oh yes! I'm feastin' on the manna*
> *from a bountiful supply . . .*

When I returned in my middle age to find this place, I expected everything to have changed. I expected new houses, perhaps even the place name, "Mount Zion," to have disappeared. But time had stood still. It was almost exactly as I remembered it. The Holiness Church was still in control of the land, and neither they nor the land had perceptibly changed. I was grateful to them, even though involuntarily my mind replayed a parody of the lines of the hymn, "Onward, Christian Soldiers." The original lyric is, *Like a mighty army/moves the church of God./Brothers we are treading/where the saints have trod.* The parody goes, *Like a mighty turtle/moves the church of God./Brothers, we are treading/where we've always trod.*

HICKORY trees at Mount Zion still shade the long slope of hill; a path still leads through deserted fields to the creek. There, just across the gravel road, is the house where I lived when I was five.

• • •

I am standing in the doorway. Behind me is the back porch. The sun is hot and bright on the gravel of the yard. There are a few chickens walking their jerky walk, watching the ground. I am a child.

The chickens talk softly among themselves, a gentle clucking, and they rattle the gravel as they scratch it with their feet, each with one bright eye at a time watching for bugs or stray kernels lost among the pebbles from the morning rain of corn thrown from Mama's hand.

• • •

I am a woman, a stranger to the occupants of the house; I ask, may I go to the backyard? — I used to live here. Really, they say. Yes, I say. *When?* they ask. A long time ago, I answer. I go to the back yard. A snapshot, double exposure.

• • •

There is the back porch, freshly painted. There are no chickens. There is green grass. There is the unpainted wood back porch, there are the chickens, there is the gravely scrubby yard. There is a hickory tree, and shade. There is nowhere a chicken house. There, beneath the hickory tree, in the shade, there is a rooster and six white hens, and a white feather caught in a wire fence. Right there, there — beside the falling down chicken house that isn't there.

• • •

I am woman, watching a child watching a woman watching a child.

• • •

THE tabernacle is gone, but the great old trees around it spread their branches above the green grass to make an even lovelier tabernacle of air and shade. There are signs I don't remember from childhood: ranging from the verse from Proverbs, IN ALL THY WAYS ACKNOWLEDGE HIM/AND HE SHALL DIRECT THY PATHS, to the attempt by some contemporary verse maker, SATAN TREMBLES WHEN HE SEES/THE WEAKEST CHRISTIAN ON HIS KNEES.

I feel the presence of Mama. Where possibly could a woman go, a single mother with two children, in 1938? Her parents were penniless in a socialist colony in Louisiana. Her father, the storekeeper, had no formal education, but he was a man of ideas, of passionate convictions. He was brave and opinionated and utterly without business sense. He signed a bank note for a friend, lost everything, gave up and took his wife to a utopian colony where they were without possessions of their own.

My mother married my father even though he was nine years younger than herself, married him as much, she would later admit, to solve the poverty problem as anything else. The year before their marriage she had dropped out of nurses training. The training was free in exchange for a woman's work in a hospital, but uniforms were required, and she had no money to buy a uniform. "There was nothing for me to do. My folks were so poor, they couldn't support me. I couldn't go home," she said. "Cleve was good looking, and I don't know — I guess I thought it might work out." When it didn't "work out," she did what women in other cultures, in other times, have done; she fled to the church for refuge.

I walked slowly past the house at the top of the hill where I was born, and circled the house at the bottom of the drive to which we returned when I was five. I allowed myself to be in several times at once, went to the creek and sat on the stones where I had sat face to face with a crawdad, and first became myself. Then I went to the Mount Zion school office, to ask questions.

I WAS directed to the woman who "had been there the longest time." She was dressed in a long, cotton dress with sleeves to her wrists in the burning August weather. Her straight, gray hair was long, fastened in a bun at the back of her neck. She was a science teacher in the Holiness school; she had been teaching there throughout her adult life. I did not say a family name, but told her that my mother once lived in a house at the top of the hill in 1934 and in the farmhouse at the bottom of the hill for a couple of years starting in 1938. She said she came to board at the school as a child ten years old, and she doubted she would remember my mother. She looked around, then, at the buildings of the school, as if she were seeing them years and years before, and said in her lovely Ozark drawl that she did remember a woman named Lelah, who had a little girl named Patsy. "I remember them, she said, because I thought Patsy was the most beautiful name in the world. She was smaller than me, but we played together some. I named my doll after her. I still have the doll, and it's still named 'Patsy.'"

"I'm Patsy," I said, and almost did not feel strange, saying it.

As I left Mount Zion, there was an old, old woman sitting on the porch swing of a house beside the road. I stopped my car, got out, walked up to her. She continued to swing slowly, her expression changing not the tiniest bit, as is the custom of ancient country women who hold court on their porch swings. I told her my name. She said hers was Zella Graybeel Buchanan. All three names rang familiar. I told her I was Lelah Vought's daughter, and asked if she remembered Lelah Vought. She thought a minute, and said, "Yes, I do. She lived over at Mount Zion. Had two little kids." She looked at me sharply: my city clothes, my shiny rental Buick. "She used to peddle eggs and things up and down this road."

Ah, Mama. You never told me that.

Wake Up Laughing

LELAH AT EIGHTEEN: 1922

In this one you are young.
You stand on a tree stump
laughing. There is sun
light on your hair. In this one
you have not been saved
at a Baptist tent revival.
You are not religious. You
have not cut off the beads
from your favorite party dress
nor pulled your long hair back
into a bun. In this one
you have not decided that you are
too tall, too bold, too worldly.

You have not yet decided that
the boy who stands beside you
is a sinner. You have not yet
given back his ring. He is the boy
you will dream about
after you are eighty, but
in this snapshot you are happy.
You have not yet been converted.

13

NAOMI wanted me to go with her to "her psychic." I love Naomi, and usually she has very good ideas. But this one gave me pause. I was past fifty, I had lived a long time without ever visiting a psychic. Trying to be polite, I put it off, neglected the suggestion; in fact, without actually saying so, I refused. For one thing, it would cost me seventy dollars; for another thing, I don't *believe* in psychics, and for a third thing . . .

But I have more than once ended up doing what Naomi wants me to do. And after all, shouldn't a person go to a psychic *once* in her life? I mean, just for the experience? I mean, just as an educational venture? And what's seventy dollars for a once-in-a-lifetime educational experience?

We went, of course. Naomi prepared me by telling me that the "being" with whom the psychic communicates is always the same "being," a spirit who refers to herself as "The Ones." It was an unseasonably warm day in February; we had made an appointment. We had two questions prepared: Naomi was going to ask what she and I had been to each other "in a former life." (I also don't believe in former lives. It's not that I *dis*believe in psychics and former lives and crystals and mantras and such — I just don't actively *believe* in them. It was so painful getting rid of the belief system I had accumulated in half a lifetime as a Christian, I have eschewed taking up any alternative beliefs. I like it, just walking through the world *not knowing*. It's so clear, somehow. So clean and uncluttered and uncomplicated.) Anyway, Naomi was going to ask what we were to each other in a former life, the reality of which she appears to accept, and I was going to ask for a message from my lost grandmother. The one who had said to me in a dream, *"What I have to offer you is Native American."*

The psychic met us at the door. She was completely unremarkable, simply dressed. My surprise told me that I must have secretly expected exotica, palm leaves, tea leaves, parrots, cards, dark skirts, brilliant blouses, crystal balls, dimmed lights, even though Naomi had told me this psychic is unpretentious. The woman who opened the door was disarmingly unpretentious. Her hair, cut short, was a little tousled; her skirt and blouse were what any woman might wear around the house. She was a middle-aged housewife, at home. She seated us around a huge coffee table made from an old wooden cable spool, got out a tape recorder, and with a few words of introduction, called for silence, closed her eyes, and apparently went into a trance. The voice that spoke to us then was brighter, touched with accent (touched also, I thought, with pretension).

"And who is this?" she asked, meaning me. Naomi introduced me. Turning slightly toward Naomi, eyes still closed, the psychic said in the altered voice, delighted now, "Ah! Our Naomi! How *are* you, our Naomi?"

Well, this seemed purely silly to me; it did not put me into a mood of significant expectation, and I had paid seventy dollars for the experience. I decided, however, by an act of will to cooperate; I would give this experience every chance to be meaningful. I would be respectful. I was there to learn.

It was my turn first. The psychic — or perhaps, "The Ones," asked me what my question was. I said that I would like to make contact with my grandmother. I did not say which grandmother. She asked the grandmother's name.

"Elzina Lakey," I said.

"And when did she pass over?" she asked.

"Do you mean, when did she die?" I was innocent of the implications of language here.

There was a slight hesitation. "Yes, in your manner of speaking," the voice was bemused. "When did she pass over from your form of life?"

"Sometime in the 1950s," I said flatly.

The voice called for silence. Then whispered, as if into vast space, "Elzina . . . Elzina Lakey . . . Elzina . . . " Then the psychic sat up more straight, as if listening, and said, "Yes. Yes." And then, to me, "She wants you to do something for her. She wants you to help bring a resolution between herself and your mother."

IT was as if I had been "slapped upside the head with a ball bat," as they used to say in rural Missouri. *Mama*? Help bring resolution to the relationship between my father's mother and *Mama*? Here I am, calling up the dead grandmother whose name I never even knew because Mama cut that family off when I was four years old — and the message is, I'm supposed to work to heal the alienation between those two old women? Give me a break!

The psychic's voice was clipping along as if she had not just overturned my own psychic can of worms; on and on she was going about how it would be *advantageous* and *beneficial* and how my grandmother could not get on with her journey until this matter was settled.

MY mother had died a year earlier, the previous February. At the moment of our visit to the psychic, her body was still lying on some sort of slab in Worcester waiting to be dissected by medical students: her own desire for the body she no longer inhabited. She made the arrangements herself — she bought a grave, bought a stone, gave her body to a medical school, and told me I wouldn't have to do anything but bury the ashes of what was left when the medical students were finished, and did I mind doing that. She said she would have taken care of that herself, too, but couldn't seem to find a way. Whatever message she intended, the message I received was hurtful and I believed she intended it to hurt. There was no funeral; when she died the body was taken immediately to Worcester, to the medical school. I didn't know when there would be ashes.

THE psychic paused for breath.

"Wait a minute," I said. "I have trouble with this message. I don't think there's anything I can do . . . "

"Oh, she doesn't want you to *do* anything — just giving some thought to the possibility of a reconciliation between them will be *very beneficial*."

I had trouble staying in the room. Later, listening to the tape, I would determine that I had said nothing to indicate that the grandmother I wanted to reach was my father's mother, as opposed to Mama's mother. I would reflect: she probably intuited, probably "read" my mind. But it would be difficult for me to believe that she had "read from my mind" the idea of a painful history between the two women, because at that moment I myself did not know the history. The grandmother was a shadowy figure of whom Mama spoke condescendingly, but with what she intended as some kindness. "Poor thing. She couldn't even read and write. It was Harv who signed her name, underneath her 'X'. Poor thing." Or, "Poor thing, she had a nervous breakdown and was in a mental hospital. Poor thing." Or, "They were so poor, dirt poor, they just lived in a little log cabin with a dirt floor. And that Harv, he was no good! He made life miserable for her! Poor thing." The idea of a reconciliation between them implied a relationship between them that I had never imagined. I was so surprised by this development, it *seemed* to come from outside myself.

I was unnerved. This experience was getting out of control. I felt tears rise, and fought to keep them down. I felt like a child, asked once again, this time from beyond the grave, to be responsible for the emotional lives of my adult (supposed) caretakers. What I felt was outrage.

The psychic went on, rambling about Elzina getting on with her journey, and how I am a writer (this the psychic could have guessed) and how Elzina would direct my pen (I was not enchanted with the idea). Since no mention was being made of a Native American connection, and I was unsettled and impatient, I told the psychic how I had dreamed, in the week following Mama's death, that Elzina appeared and announced, "What I have to offer you is Native American."

The psychic took off after that like a dog after a bone. She was delighted. She lapsed rhapsodic about great flaming sunsets and vast skies. I was highly skeptical; in southern Missouri the skies are cupped by Ozark mountains; oak trees, hills, break the skyline all around. The pictures she was painting sounded to me like Arizona. Vast skies. Flaming sunsets. She said Elzina wanted me to know that I must find my name. Feeling myself dangerously slipping toward a foggy romanticism, I asked, "Does she mean, my 'Indian name'?" I had told a friend named Joan Mallonee about my dream of my grandmother, and Joan had said, smiling enigmatically, "You must find your Indian name." I didn't believe in having an "Indian name" but then I didn't believe in psychics, either, and here I was, asking questions of one. My negative attitude toward white women taking on Indian names was intensified the second summer I led a writing workshop on a wilderness river trip with Anne Dellenbaugh. A participant on that trip said her name was "She Goat," and said she was a shaman. "Anyone," she said, "can become a shaman in forty-five minutes."

"Yes." The psychic said, almost whispering. "Your Indian name. Yes."

Then she held up a hand. "Wait." And listened. "She is saying something. She says, 'Just let me hold my baby. Please. Just let me hold my baby.'"

It came out of nowhere. It was like an electric shock. It broke the facade of my dismissal of what was happening. At some significant level, it disturbed.

Later, Leona, Elzina's daughter, would tell me that Elzina walked many times to the filling station owned by my Aunt Nellie and Uncle Elmer. She told them that she knew I was visiting them, and that she was my grandmother. She asked to see me. And they turned her away. She did this repeatedly. Repeatedly, she was turned away. Later, when I heard that story, I would remember the strange voice saying *"Let me hold my baby. Just let me hold my baby."* And I would say in my heart that I don't know what to believe. I don't know what is real, and what is imagined, what is dream, what is myth, what is genius, what is silliness, what is story, what is true and everlasting. I don't understand what time is, what death is, who God is. I suspect they are mixed up together, like dreaming. I will never be able to sort it out. But I do wish my Aunt Nellie had said yes to my grandmother when I was a four-year-old girl in rural Missouri.

When it was Naomi's turn, the psychic answered her question, "What were we to one another in a former life," with a long, intense tale that left me breathless with admiration for the psychic's storytelling power, whether she in fact got the tale from someone who had — quote — passed over — unquote — or not. I would love to have her participate in one of my creative writing workshops. She said Naomi and I were sisters in a land where there were terrible wars, and someone murdered our mother and cut the head from the body parts, and dumped the head and the body, disconnected, at our feet. We were young, she said, but not that young — and inconsolable. She traced our lives from one disaster to another, until finally we wandered out in a desert together, preferring (she said) to die together than either of us going on alone. She said she would tell us other lives but it would require other sessions. The thought flashed through my mind: seventy dollars per previous life. And then I was a little ashamed of my skepticism.

As the session drew to an end, the psychic said there were others crowding in, wanting to make contact. (*Too bad we haven't time today. Other sessions, other dollars?*) One, she said, was an Indian man. Tall, very tall. Very impressive. She said he wanted me to know that he was a very important man. He knew when to plant corn, when it would grow best. I had an image of great self-importance; male macho beyond the grave. It felt comic to me. She said he was asking if I would return to Missouri. I said yes, in fact I would be going in August. He said he would meet me there. The psychic said she would help me by making it specific, and asked me to name a place. My mind went to the lonely place where I went as a child when we visited Aunt Nellie and Uncle Elmer: a deep cut in an abandoned road, made by the army to block passage into Fort Leonard Wood. A cut blasted and left raw, where I could descend into the earth and touch fossils; life lived millions of years ago; my ancestors, the creatures who swam there in vanished seas.

I felt myself again that child. Suddenly I wanted to believe, in spite of myself. "Ask him," I said, "if he will meet me in the cut in the rock." The old biblical and hymn words washed through my mind: *hide my soul in the cleft of the rock"* and

> *The shadow of a mighty rock within a weary land*
> *A home within the wilderness, a rest upon the way*
> *From the burning of the noontide heat*
> *and the burden of the day.*

"He says you need to go there by yourself," she said, after whispering the question I had asked, and waiting for an answer. "But he will meet you when you come out of that place."

Wake Up Laughing

Strange, I thought, how right that feels. I do want to go to the cut in the rock. And I want to go alone. I do not want to share it, even with the *possibility* of a prideful, macho, Indian, corn-growing ghost. Even if he *is* an ancestor. Even if . . .

"Ask him," I said to the psychic, "if he will tell me my Indian name."

She whispered the question. Waited. Nodded. "He says yes. When you leave that place, he will tell you your name."

14

IN March, shortly after my day with Naomi at the psychic's, while the ground was still frozen, the medical school in Worcester called and said they were finished with the body of Mama; we could pick up the ashes whenever we wished. I asked Sam to go get them, and he did. On my birthday, June 1st, I buried them.

I had told my husband and children when this would happen, and assured them that they should feel perfectly free to join me or not. They chose not to, and I was glad. If she loved them, she had peculiar ways of showing it. For my oldest daughters especially, love for her was mixed with pain. We gathered in my living room immediately after her death; we told stories, prayed, and sang as my son Paul played her favorite hymns on the piano. We remembered her laughter, her intense interests in politics and history. We remembered her tenderly, and we blessed her. It seemed a meaningful and a sufficient closure.

As I was preparing to bury the ashes, my youngest daughter chose to go with me. I did not want to officially open the grave. To do so would cost several hundred dollars and there would be grave diggers and a truck standing by while I buried three cups of white ash and bone fragment. The week before was Memorial Day. I chose June 1st because it was my birthday, because it turned out to be a beautiful day, and because I figured everyone would be finished at the cemetery, and no one would notice a new geranium planted on a grave.

When Mama was old, suffering fracture after fracture from osteoporosis, my youngest daughter was a little girl. She read books aloud, lying on the bed beside her grandmother. They giggled together; they shared a playful sense of humor. They loved each other, and Mama was not critical of her as she had been of my older daughters.

We bought geraniums, and then drove together the forty-five minute trip to Sam and Eve's house. The air was heavy with the scent of springtime; mountain laurel was in bloom, white clouds of blossoms seeming to float in the open spaces between trees in the New England woods. We rode with the car windows open, speaking hardly at all. We were remembering Mama and breathing the deeply sweet, warm air.

Sam put a small white box, smaller than a shoe box but surprisingly heavy, in my hands. He hesitated, almost going with us, then waved us good-by.

We drove the forty-five minutes back to the cemetery near my home. We were silent. Evening was coming down gently.

In the cemetery, it was as I expected. Most of the graves were beautifully decorated; there was no one to be seen. The house of the cemetery keeper was dark, the shades drawn, the windows closed. My daughter and I found the grave that Mama had purchased, the stone she had ordered with her name carved on it. I said I needed to go behind some bushes for a minute to relieve myself before we began the serious work of burial. I started to do so, but my daughter laughed, "That's a grave!" and as I moved, embarrassed, "She'd like that! She's probably laughing, right now!"

A little disoriented by the fracture in the calm of the evening and by the enormity of burying my mother, I picked up the shovel and started to push it into the dirt.

"That's the wrong grave!"

Pat Schneider

We found the right grave, and my daughter's voice was gentle as she suggested, "Lets just sit down and be quiet for a little while."

We sat down on the earth. The fireflies were brilliant, transient stars among the trees of that old hillside cemetery. We let silence gather, and seriousness. I held the box of ashes in my hands, and listened to the June evening.

Suddenly, in the silence, we heard voices approaching. My husband, our oldest daughter, and her eight-year-old daughter had changed their minds. They had come to join us. At first I felt a twinge of disappointment; we had just entered what felt like a centered, still place in which I could bury the ashes of Mama. But I said to myself, *let it be.* And the stillness opened up, and received the other three people. We sat together, then, around the unbroken grave, and sang again the song she had requested, that ended, *it is well, it is well, with my soul.* My husband took the shovel and opened the earth. The black, rich soil. I opened the box. The ashes bone white in the twilight. I lifted one small bone fragment and laid it on the cut earth, where it shone brilliant white. Then each of us, including my granddaughter with her mother's help, took a little ash and sprinkled it into the dark earth. At last it was my youngest daughter's turn, whom Mama had loved purely. She shifted, knelt on both knees, dipped both hands deeply, fully, into the ash, lifted a full measure, both hands filled, and poured it into the little grave. I poured out what remained, and before we covered it, I recited a long section of a poem by James Russell Lowell that Mama had recited to me every June 1st, on my birthday, which begins:

> *And what is so rare as a day in June?*
> *Then, if ever, come perfect days*
> *When heaven tries earth, if it be in tune,*
> *And over it softly her warm ear lays . . .*

Wake Up Laughing

We closed the earth, sang a final song, and then I said I wanted to be alone for a little while. My family walked away down the hill. The silence was deep; night had quieted even the last of the birds.

I said softly, "Mama, I have done everything you asked me to do. Your body went to the medical school. I have buried your ashes. We sang the song you asked us to sing. I don't know anything more to do."

I waited. Nothing more came to mind. The night was very still. Then I said, "Now, Mama. I want to ask something of you. I ask you to talk to Elzina Lakey." Then I looked up into the shadowy shapes of trees, and said, "Elzina, I want you to know that Mama never spoke unkindly of you."

Then I said, "Now it's up to the two of you. I have done all that I know to do."

At that instant the most awful noise erupted in a nearby tree — two animals screeching and screaming — the quiet evening exploded. A huge branch of the tree was in motion, waving and swaying, as a terrible racket went on and on.

I was sincerely trying to be deep and meditative and profound; I was trying to be what the psychic had called "advantageous" and "beneficial"; she said I should just quietly *visualize* a meeting. I tried to ignore the ruckus in the trees, and meditate on Mama meeting my grandmother, but quickly the whole thing felt silly to me, and I gave up, got up from the ground where I sat, and walked down the hill.

My youngest daughter walked back to meet me. She whispered. "Did you hear *that*?"

The noise had stopped, as suddenly as it began.

I laughed, and said, "Yeah, what do you think they were? It sounded like two different animals — a raccoon, maybe? And something else?"

When we caught up with her, Rebecca said, "One was a possum — I saw it. A raccoon and a possum."

Before I joined them, my daughters had said to each other that the voice of the animal was their grandmother. The thought had not occurred to me. I don't particularly believe or disbelieve in psychics. What I do believe in is the genius of the human mind — its ability to intuit, to imagine, to create. Nevertheless, even though it does not fit the Protestant theology I was raised on, nor even the lovely cleared space my present consciousness has won from traditional beliefs — nevertheless, those two animals did sound like two old women with a lifetime of fury to vent. It must have done them both a lot of good.

15

MAMA

Kerosene, gasoline, Maybelline, Vaseline —
Mama said she knew a family in the Ozark mountains
named their baby Vaseline Malaria
because the words were pretty.
Mama's dead now seven years, and I don't visit
the shallow grave where she wanted her ashes buried.
The one time I did walk there alone,
a big, black dog stood guard,
his legs braced far apart, fur
on his neck rising.

Mama was powerful. Even when she wobbled
with her walker down the nursing home hall,
Mama was powerful.
Where does all that power go when the body falls,

Pat Schneider

when it is reduced to ashes?
Does the power linger in the minds of the bereaved?
Are we bereaved?

Or are we criss-crossed with contradiction?

Do we just happen to walk into the cemetery
at the random moment when the sun is going down
and the young woman who lives in the house
on the cemetery land lets her guard dog run?
Do we happen to be on his territory as shadows
are growing behind stones and beneath trees?
Is it simply animal fear, animal protection,
that brings him looming, growling to the brink
of a shallow grave, the warning
in his throat as deep as wilderness?

Or is it power that has been set free
and has no where to go?

I remember Mama by lamplight in the smell of kerosene.
I remember her fingers touching the dime store counter, Maybelline.
I can see her in the doorway of the filling station
where her sister kept the books
and her sister's husband pumped gasoline.
I hear her voice repeating and repeating the story
about the people who named their baby pretty words:
Vaseline.
Malaria.

Wake Up Laughing

I keep moving her passion back, wanting it to stay
back there in those things. Seven years, and still
I do not walk in the cemetery. Still
I do not visit her grave. Still
the black dog stands guard at the edges of my mind.
This is mine! he says. *Don't come here!*
The voice is Mama's.

16

I ARRIVED in Waynesville at one o'clock. The town is without charm. An adjunct to Fort Leonard Wood, the town itself is an army surplus issue. Depressing. What I can remember of it from my childhood is a little better, but not much. There was a square. In New England they are called commons, and many of them aren't square. In the Midwest they are square, and they are called what they are — square.

When I was a child, the square in Waynesville had trees and a small, brick courthouse. Now it has a big, ugly, "modern" courthouse, a dilapidated gazebo moved, crowded, onto a corner, and one tree. A highway is the spine of the town, bordered on one side with an awkward sidewalk three feet higher than the asphalt, reachable by climbing crumbling concrete steps. Edging the sidewalk, a tiny cafe sells BLTs and cheeseburgers — the kind of place where everyone stops talking when you walk in because you're the most interesting and unusual thing they've seen in a while and apparently some significance is attached to what you order, what you wear, how you speak. Everyone else is "Joe," "Ellie," "Maryanne," or "Hey, Fella." *You* are "Ma'am."

I sat for an hour lingering over my BLT-on-toasted-wheat-bread-thank-you, looking out the window at the ugly new courthouse, listening to the English language spoken as I first learned it, as I have not often heard it in my adult life. It was like hearing a lullaby that you thought you had completely forgotten. Deeply familiar, strangely sweet.

IT was a large thing that I was going to do — walk across the asphalt highway, enter the courthouse, put a coin in the public telephone and call a woman I had not seen for fifty three years. The only living person who knew my father when he was young. When he was my father. His sister, Leona.

I ATE the BLT slowly. Sipped the Diet Pepsi slowly. The regulars lost interest in me. "Hey, Fella — you git that ole junk back on th' road, or what?" Nods, gestures. They all knew the answers to the questions. Coffee and a donut brought to a customer without asking what he wanted. The waitress grinned at him. She was young, to be missing so many teeth.

17

THE first time I dialed the number at the wall phone in the courthouse, I got a busy signal. And the second time. And the third. *She's talking to a daughter*, I thought. *I am the subject,* I thought. The courthouse was new enough to seem a little raw inside. No one in sight. A wide corridor. Closed doors. A display of pictures on a revolving rack: Pulaski County around 1900. Serious faces. Poor, wooden houses. Families standing in a self-conscious line beside farm animals, wagons. Sepia landscapes. Vanished histories.

BEFORE I dialed again I stood silently at the wall phone. *She will answer this time*, I thought. *I will say, "Aunt Leona?" Dear God.*

I allowed myself to feel Mama's voice. All those years, all those times. "Promise me you will never have anything to do with them. They are so poor. They are so ignorant. They will just be a burden to you. Promise me."

"I promise, Mama."

I dialed the number. A voice said, "Hello?"

"Aunt Leona?"

I waited for her under the one tree at the corner of the square. Oak. All over Missouri, Oak. Hickory. Hardy stuff, climbing up the hot air, out of

Wake Up Laughing

the rocky Ozark earth. I stood under the oak tree for the same reason cattle huddled under oak in fields along the highway. The shade, minor mercy in that heavy heat. I stood with my back to the courthouse and the pathetic gazebo, my face toward the rental car I had described to Leona on the telephone. Wine-colored, I had said. Rental, I had said. Standing in a line with several old giants parked beside the square, my car looked far too shiny, far too new, much too Buick. Even in the center of town, the heat seemed to throb in the rhythm, the pulse, of grasshoppers.

Waiting, my mind rearranged the stores, put the Greyhound Bus sign back on the squat building on the corner across the street from where I stood, and there I was, thirteen years old, and there was my Uncle Elmer, helping me onto the bus sending me home to St. Louis. My mother's mother was dying that summer, and we rode the bus back and forth to Waynesville, helping care for her in the back room of Aunt Nellie's filling station. I was never to talk to strangers. I was to play only behind the station, because my father's family lived nearby, and they might see me. Mama said I could look through the keyhole, once, to see my father in the filling station. He was laughing, and drinking a Royal Crown. Uncle Elmer put me, by myself, on the bus to St. Louis — there, right there across the street in front of that squat building, pressing a silver dollar into my hand, telling me, "Don't mention this to Nellie." And Aunt Nellie was back at the filling station, ringing up bills for gas, for bread, for crackers and sardines at the counter where the candy bars behind her glowed and promised.

And so I was startled when a voice behind me said, "Patsy?"

I turned, and there was a woman, tall as I am tall, her face so similar to my own that I might have been meeting myself in another life. She had tears in her eyes.

"Yes," I said. "Aunt Leona?"

Leona

Cleve and Tom Vogt

Cleve

Patsy. Given to me by Leona, the only
photograph my father or his family had of me.

Linnie *Patsy*

*Harv with my daddy's "other little girl," Sharon
and Leona's daughter, Bernice*

Leona holding Elzina and Harv's wedding photograph

Leona holding the only picture of the Dutch ancestors — and the cigarette that is causing her death from emphysema

Mama, whose name was Lelah

Samuel

Sam Vought

The green and white sign in southern Missouri

Mt. Zion Holiness community sign

Where the tabernacle stood at Mt. Zion

The creek at Mt. Zion

The corner where we lived in St. Louis, and the dome of the cathedral

The block where we lived in St. Louis

The church in St. Louis

The cornflowers in the empty lot in St. Louis

The Protestant church ruin at Dún Lúiche, Ireland

Máire O'Donohoe

Me, at the old Quaker cemetery at Moat, Ireland

18

LEONA lives in a trailer. "House trailer," we called them when I was a child in Missouri. That year at Boiling Springs, Mama bought a small house trailer for one hundred dollars and had it parked in the yard of the one-room school. She taught; Sam was in second grade and I was in third grade and somehow I knew she suffered loneliness and confusion. Years later, if that year was mentioned, she would say, "I didn't know how to teach — they didn't learn a thing that year." And there was the little boy who became very ill and afterwards was completely deaf, and she grieved, not knowing what to do, not knowing how to teach him.

For me the year was good because I fell in love with the ice on the edges of the creek, and the water — its music; and the rocks; and the mystery of the way the creek itself disappeared among the trees. How it was alive, and restless, and incredibly beautiful.

I know something about living in a house trailer. The bad part is how hot, how cold, how cramped you are. The good part is how the outside is closer to the inside. You are almost outside. Outside leans toward you — night noises, daytime throb of grasshoppers, even heat and cold, even death by hunger or exposure — more real, more present, closer in. The outside listening, speaking constantly. So your dreams get more mixed up with moonlight and your habits get more in keeping with the rising and setting of the sun. It's a smaller shell around your life than a whole house, and somewhere in your nervous system you know it, and so you listen more and you are afraid more and when the water sings in and out of its ice palaces in the little rocky creek, you rejoice more. Because not having so many other things to watch, you see the ice. You hear the water.

At least if you are eight years old you do. If your mother's suffering is off there, up there where adults think and worry and remember. At least that's the way I imagine it was, remember it, standing fifty years in the future.

19

LEONA sat on one of the two decaying overstuffed chairs on her porch. Gray stuffing lay visible, bulged out of the split arms of the chairs. The porch was a rough, wooden platform attached to an ancient house trailer.

Inside, every inch of space was used. An old couch, a small TV, a little table crowded with cereal boxes, instant coffee, sugar, a pint fruit jar filled with teaspoons. At her feet a brown terrier tumbled with excitement and she quieted him with a few words and an indulgent grin. He was not a young dog, but his name was "Pup." One of the first things she had said when we entered the door was, "I just don't know what would happen to Pup, if anything happened to me."

She coughed often. Later, when I asked about the cough, she answered flatly, in a tone of understatement and vast resignation, "Emphysema. And cancer, too, they say. Ain't nothin' they can do, and them nicotine patches, they cost too much. Nobody can afford that." Beyond the table a bed sheet was strung neatly across the trailer to make a private space behind it.

She balanced a mug of coffee in one hand, a cigarette in the other. "I never did know what happened to them," she said softly, not looking at me. I wasn't looking at her, either. We were awkward with one another, a bare half hour into our first meeting after a lifetime apart.

She was talking about Cleve, her brother. She was talking about my father. And Mama. "I never did know what happened to them."

"You mean," I asked, "why they split up?"

She nodded, still looking past the unpainted two-by-four that supported her porch. She repeated, "I never did know what happened." Grasshoppers throbbed in the silence. She was clearly asking whether I knew.

I sipped coffee from the mug she had handed me inside the trailer, where I had first sat uneasily on the edge of the old couch, Pup excitedly circling in the tiny space, a hundred or more knickknacks crowding every shelf, every windowsill, every top of every surface, their little messages: *"I love grandma," "Lake of the Ozarks."* And dim old pictures of her ancestors. My ancestors. On the walls.

This moment on the porch was the first test. Would we be honest with each other, or would we ease around the hard questions, the hard answers?

I swallowed the coffee, looked into the mug, began slowly. "Well, of course all I have is Mama's side of the story. It may not be fair."

She was silent, a long, thin line of smoke rising in the August heat from the little wand in her right hand.

"Mama said he liked other women. She said he went to other women. She said he would leave, and say he was never coming back, and then he *would* come back."

Leona smiled. Nodded. "That sound's 'bout like Cleve, alright," she said softly. "He liked to run around."

I eased back into my chair. I liked this woman. And we were going to tell the truth.

20

WHEN we were little, Mama took us to Wichita, Kansas, because there was work for women there making airplanes for the war in Europe. She rented a tiny house which was partially finished, on a lot that had not been seeded for grass. The rooms were mostly bare because we couldn't afford furniture, and the yard was dirt when the sun was hot, mud when it rained. She sharpened drill bits at the factory. She was not meant to be a mother. She read. She lost herself in books on science and history and politics. She loved the poems she had learned as a child in school, and music — especially music she couldn't understand. She was her father's daughter: dreamer, visionary, prophet. She should never have been "Mama."

CYCLONE

The night the cyclone ripped
around the house, big oaks
and sycamores went down
on all four sides. I remember
Mama happy, then, for days.
Almost as if that's what she'd like to do —

Wake Up Laughing

tear up a lot of trees without hurting anyone,
and then, before the daylight came,
simply disappear.

In another lifetime, or in the one
she had, but in another sex,
she would have been inventor,
discoverer, anything but "Mama."

She made hominy out in the yard:
black belly of the cast iron pot,
hot coals, her attentive hover.
She made lye soap out there, too,
drew water up ninety-seven feet and
gave it to the goat, because the goat
was more particular than the cow,
and wouldn't drink at all
if there was Jersey drool
in the watering trough.

Mama made hominy once.
She made lye soap once.
She canned corn on the cob, once, too,
just to see if she could do it.

Nothing that turned out good
was ever done again.

In Wichita, Sam was seven and a half, and I was nine years old. She would go to work and leave us alone, and when she'd come back he would be gone. She said he was running away. That's what she said about our father, too; she left him because he kept "running off." And so there was a primal danger in "Samuel running away."

I think he simply wandered down the street looking for someone to play with. I wasn't much fun. I was into reading Terhune's dog books, and he was in the second grade and not interested in second grade books, Dick and Jane. I don't remember that she ever had a lot of trouble finding him, but it frightened her, and she kept saying she had to do something about it.

He had one toy that he loved like some kids love a stuffed animal or a blanket. It was a metal vehicle, a white milk truck that had real rubber wheels on metal axles that turned, and he would lay on his belly playing with it, making the engine noises little boys make, his yellow hair in the sunlight like a flower out behind the house in that packed-dirt Kansas yard. He was seven years old, but the truck had been his favorite for a long time, and he still called it by a baby name: *Eedle Deedle*. He would say it over and over, imitating the bell on the milk truck that in those days drove slowly up and down streets, ringing a bell for housewives to come out and buy a bottle of milk.

Mama took hold of him one day and told him in a very serious tone of voice, "Samuel," — she said she named him Samuel because of its Biblical meaning, but she told me as a secret that she didn't want him when he was born; by that time she already knew that our father was just no good. She said the first time she loved Samuel was when he was five days old and circumcised, and the membrane holding his tongue down was cut, so he was bleeding at both ends and screaming as my father and the doctor looked on and laughed. Then, she said, she knew she loved her baby boy. "Samuel," she said to him in that serious tone of voice, "if you ever, if you *ever* run away again, I will take a hammer and I will smash Eedle Deedle. I won't want to, but I will. I will pound Eedle Deedle and I will throw him away. Do you understand?"

Wake Up Laughing

He said he understood.

The next day he ran away.

Mama believed in keeping her word. She let maggots grow in the dishrag on the kitchen counter; she forgot about washing and mending clothes; she didn't like to clean, but Mama believed in keeping her word.

She had given her word that she would destroy Eedle Deedle. Samuel was out in the yard, and he started screaming when she first pulled Eedle Deedle from his arms. I couldn't watch. I felt sick. I went inside and listened to his screaming and listened to the sound of the hammer on the painted white metal sides of Eedle Deedle. The screaming stopped before the pounding did. Then it was silent. She brought Samuel into the house, then, and told us how it hurt her more than it did him, and she cried. Neither Samuel nor I felt like crying anymore. He was very still, and what I felt was dead calm. We had to comfort her.

Then she went back out into the weeds where she had thrown Eedle Deedle and she brought him out and said she was sorry, and she'd fix him. She pulled and pulled at him with the hammer hooks, and pounded, but Eedle Deedle was gone. Samuel was patting her and telling her not to cry, that he was glad she did it, that she did right. But it didn't make any difference. He just kept on running away and running away and running away.

• • •

When I was a child and the yard was a field of mud and Mama pounded my brother's favorite toy with a hammer until it was no longer a white, metal truck, and then cried, and we comforted her . . .

When I was a child and my brother was seven, and he could not cry for his only love, his Eedle Deedle, because he had to comfort his mother, who was crying . . .

Pat Schneider

When I was a child, I became an adult.

On that day in the summer of my ninth year I became an adult because I clearly saw — I saw and understood — that Mama was a child and there was nothing, no one, between me and the abyss. There was nothing, no one who could save us — myself, my brother, or Mama — from the dark suck of mud in the yard of that dismal house in Kansas. Nothing that would stand between my brother and destruction. Nothing, no one, unless it was me.

In that moment I understood myself to be unmothered and unfathered.

I turned, then, and spread out over my brother the great eagle wings of my intention. I became mother to Mama and fierce warrior protector of my brother. And the little girl who had been there before, went away.

• • •

21

The 1932 Chevy sits in the yard of the little house, propped up on makeshift blocks, both doors open wide in the hot midsummer air. He sings a song he has heard Gene Autry sing on the radio: South of the border, down Mexico way . . . *He is happy because he has money in his pocket and he guesses it's his own damned business what he does with it — the supervisor at the cheese factory wants him to get his hernia fixed again, but he reckons it'll fix itself if he just lays low awhile. He grins, glances at the tall wire fence that separates the rocky yard of this rented house from the asphalt yard of the factory.* South of the border, *he sings again, bending to the spark plugs,* down Mexico way. That's where I fell in love when stars above came out to play . . .

Inside the car, a little girl sits on the passenger seat. She is happy, too, listening to her daddy sing. She pretends she is driving — going on a long, long road to far away. She jiggles her body a little, pretending the motion is around her. She is hot in the car, but the dashboard has numbers in a circle, and she can read some of the numbers. Her legs are so short they stick out straight in front of her, bare below her short dress. Sweaty, they stick to the seat.

He is going away. He is never coming back this time — this time he means it, he tells himself, and reaches for the grease rag he tucked into his hip pocket. Goddamned woman's nothin' but a bawl-bag — a man can't put up with a cryin' woman ever' live-long day. His song falters. Deliberately he changes the subject in his mind. Arizona, maybe. Nah — too hot. Minnesota! That's more like it. He can see the plains stretching out before him, the shining road, the vast, upturned cereal bowl of the sky at night. Yeah, he thinks. Minnesota.

The child moves carefully to release her sweaty legs from the leather seat. She leans out the open door of the car and calls, "Sing it again, Daddy!" He grins. South of the border, *he sings,* down Mexico way . . . , *happiness rising inside him with the song.*

22

"DO you want to see your Daddy?" Mama asked me one afternoon. "He's in the filling station," she said. "Would you like to see him?" She asked flat like that, simple, as if she were asking do you want a drink of water.

I didn't answer. At the time, I was taking my turn sitting beside Grandma, who was dying in a hospital bed set up in Aunt Nellie's living room. The front wall of the living room was attached to the filling station where Aunt Nellie and Uncle Elmer worked, and the back wall was attached to a house trailer by one cinder block in between for a step. Grandma was dying and there was blood for the first time between my legs. I was frightened of the rattling sound of Grandma's breathing and I didn't like the sticky bulk of cotton against my crotch. Living and dying were complicated affairs.

Do you want to see your Daddy? That's the way I remember it, but I don't think that's what she said. She never called him "your Daddy." She talked about him only as "Cleve." I believe she said, "Do you want to see Cleve?" But something in me translated it immediately to the little-girl name I had used before he went away.

People remember the place where they were when something is said that alters their lives. Shock takes a snapshot of the scene. The back rooms of Aunt Nellie's filling station — the hospital bed in the middle of the living room, the door to a house trailer pulled up against the rear of the building, the closed door to the filling station — are vivid in my mind, fused with the question, "Do you want to see your Daddy?" The question itself burned the scene into my mind.

Once, when it was my turn to sit by Grandma in the night, I had opened the back door and stepped quickly through the cold dark onto the cinder block and into the trailer that was Aunt Nellie's kitchen. I opened the refrigerator. It was completely empty except for one can of peaches. Mostly we ate out of packages from the shelves in the filling station. Sometimes we went across Highway 66 to the Silver Star Cafe. That night I ate the peaches out of the can with a fork, and drank most of the juice, but I left three slices and a little juice, so the refrigerator wouldn't be completely bare.

Cleve. I used to think about that when we had vocabulary words in the seventh grade. How he didn't cleave. How that's not the way he spelled it, but he didn't. He didn't cleave. Mama said he kept "running off." That's what she said my little brother was doing, too, before she took a long rope and tied him to an oak tree.

Do you want to see your Daddy?

I didn't answer because I didn't know what to say. "If you want to see him, you can bend down and look at him through the keyhole," she said in the tone of voice one might use for inviting a child to look at a repulsive insect. She turned to leave, as if she was finished with the conversation. I got up from my chair beside Grandma's bed, and followed her. "He's out there in the filling station," she said, and she bent down herself, just to make sure he was still there. "That's him," she whispered, not that she needed to; the filling station was long and narrow, and he was far away, the only person at the other end.

She waited while I looked for a minute, and then she said, "You can go on out there, if you want. Just remember he doesn't love you, though.

Wake Up Laughing

He never did love you. And he has another little girl now. But you can go on out there, if you want." She went back out to the kitchen and left me alone. She had done her work well. No team of horses could have pulled me out to where he was.

I bent down on my knees and pasted my face against the door. The filling station stretched out on the other side of the keyhole. Loaves of Sunbeam bread, ten cents a loaf, stacked on the low shelf that ran down the center. Boxes of Nabisco Shredded Wheat, little cans of sardines, small jars of mayonnaise and mustard. Boxes of Baby Ruth candy bars. Butterfingers. Cans of Red Dog snuff. Aunt Nellie sitting behind the cash register. Smiling. How could she smile? Didn't she know she was smiling at the enemy?

And there, leaning against the ice chest, under the sign for Royal Crown soda, was someone I once called "Daddy." A long time ago — so long ago I wasn't sure I could remember it. He was facing me, looking at my Aunt Nellie, telling a story, and laughing. All at once I had this crazy idea: I wanted to tell him. If I could tell him, maybe it wouldn't be so bad. Maybe it wouldn't be just awkward and ugly and uncomfortable. Mama said it's perfectly natural, just act like nothing happened; put on a pad and don't make a fuss about it. I wanted to know what a daddy might say. Does a daddy know when his little girl becomes a woman?

The aisle between the food shelves was long and straight between us, and he was standing exactly in the center at the end. In the light from the filling station window, his hair was the same yellow as Samuel's hair, and curly. In his hand, a bottle of pop, a Royal Crown.

23

AS if suddenly, as if in a dream, as if there was no preparation at all, there was my father's grave, between Leona and me. Years before, in the days when Naomi urged me to write about my own life, one of the first pieces I wrote was a long poem, "Olive Street Transfer," which contained these lines:

> *I walk this year in downed October leaves*
> *and think the hard and actual*
> *stone*
> *against your grave*
> *must bear your name*
> *as I do not.*
>
> *Nor do I bear, except a curl*
> *of hurt,*
> *any part of you.*
>
> *Your name,*
> *my father,*

is growing obsolete.
It does not matter so much
any more. See,
the hair I used to straighten
because it curled like yours,
I allow to curl
behind my ear.

I will go some year
before I die,
ask to see your photograph,
find your grave
and stand as close to you
as I can. I will introduce myself.

How we see, in our mind's eye, places, events, times. How I made it up, the lay of the land, the thick grass, the stately trees, myself alone and angry beside the grave of my lost father, confronting him, introducing myself as I did not dare to do that day when I was thirteen. Or on that other day, still thirteen, when Uncle Elmer waved me off on a Greyhound bus and, rolling out of town, I realized the man in the seat across the aisle and up a little way toward the front was the man I had watched through the keyhole in the back door to Aunt Nellie's filling station.

I made it up, the meeting at his grave. I would be alone; I would tell him how desperately I had wanted to say to the stranger on the bus, "*Daddy?*" How I believed he would not want me. How I believed Mama: "*He doesn't love you. He never loved you.*" How I sat in the bus seat evaluating my own adolescent face. *Pimples*, I thought. *Ugly*, I thought. *He'd be ashamed of me*, I thought. *Maybe I'm wrong; maybe it's not him,* I thought.

For three hours we rode together northeast from Waynesville to

St. Louis. He talked with other passengers, laughed, occasionally even looked briefly at the kid behind him in the aisle seat who was staring at him. He brushed his curly hair back from his forehead with the hand that had a missing finger. Proof. The missing finger was proof positive. My heart, in its cage of ribs. *My father.* I had heard the story from Mama — how he shot his finger off to get her back after she left him. In her old age, she denied that story. Said no, it was to get the attention of some other woman.

In the cemetery my father was a stranger. How hard the rocky ground. How that fist of earth was knuckled with rock, how the straggly grass struggled to grow.

On either side of his tombstone there were concrete pots of plastic flowers. *He has another little girl.* Leona told me about them. Their sorrows, their problems. Alcohol. "Terrible trouble." Jail. They are living the life I might have lived.

• • •

At the end of this visit I will stand face to face with Leona's daughter, my cousin. In blood, she is as close to me as my cousin Rozema on Mama's side, who has been almost my sister. In Leona's daughter's yard, a bunch of men and boys will throw a ball between them, as if there is not a shiny, rented Buick in their front yard. As if they don't notice the woman from the east coast who looks so much like Leona. Her daughter will tell me good-bye in carefully paced words, her Ozark accent heavy. "Sure is too bad," she will say in that slow, soft drawl, "Sure is too bad you missed so much." And I will see it: what I missed, and what I gained. What Mama feared, what she tried to save me from, what she took away from me. The grandparents, the family, the history, the love. The poverty, the alcoholism, the abuse, the desperation. I will be sad. But I will be grateful.

Wake Up Laughing

AT the foot of his grave, a flat stone engraved with identification in the U.S. Army. After the divorce, he gave his working life to the army — around the edges of the army — a short time in the service, a medical discharge for something related to his eyes, the rest of his life working as a civilian at Fort Leonard Wood.

Earlier in the afternoon, Leona told me how he suffered before he died on the operating table during his second operation for ulcers. How he lost his sense of humor. He changed, his sister said. He became so thin, so unhappy.

Standing beside his grave in the town cemetery with Leona a little to the side and behind me, I am silent. I open my camera, take a couple of pictures. It is Leona who can grieve for him. And his wife. And his other daughters. And his son, the one who "is terrible trouble." There is nothing, after all, that I can say to my father.

Nearby, down the rocky slope of the cemetery, another grave is marked with a wooden slab and the hand-lettered words: "Tom Vogt." My father's brother. The wooden slab held down by several rocks. Tucked under one, the stem of a plastic flower.

24

LEONA sat beside me on the porch of her house trailer, her legs crossed, her cigarette held carefully away from the billow of stuffing along the chair arm where the fabric had given way. The story, told in her gentle, familiar accent, was about her father and mother. My grandfather and grandmother. I wish I could capture her way of speaking. I love it, hear it in my most inner ear, but if I try to capture her exact inflection, it escapes like the breath of someone loved and lost. And how to capture Harv Vogt and Elzina Lakey — 'Zina Vogt? How they were young and poor before they were old and poor. *"Dirt poor,"* Mama said. *"So poor, and so ignorant. Why, Cleve's mother couldn't even write her own name! She signed with an X! It was Harv, had to write her name out."*

To my knowledge, Mama never once spoke to me the name of my grandmother. Elzina. Elzina Lakey Vogt. Nor did she ever speak of her as "your grandmother." She was always "Cleve's mother." Harv was "Harv," but Elzina was "Cleve's mother." Neither of them was ever called "your" anything. They were Cleve's, and I was no longer Cleve's, and they were no longer mine. When they married, she talked him into changing his name from Vogt to Vought, because she was ashamed to be associated with his people. When they divorced, he took back his original spelling,

Wake Up Laughing

but she and Sam and I, kept the new spelling. I did not even know that his name was spelled differently from my own, let alone know anything about his people.

How, then, am I to capture Elzina and Harv, this woman, this man, young in the years when this century was young — 1905, 1908, living in a religious commune because Harv was convinced that some preacher was Jesus Christ come back to earth. The preacher said that's who he was: *"I am Jesus Christ. I will never die. Work and give me all your money. I will portion it out. I will take care of you."* Harv believed. Elzina did not.

There was Elzina, not yet twenty years old, unable to read or write, saying "No." Saying "I can't take it any more." Saying "I'm leaving. I'm going home to my folks." It was 1907 or 1908; she was already mother to two of the nine children for whom she would open, bear down, give birth, give milk, watch some die, raise the rest "dirt poor" — too poor to get "any schooling to speak of."

Later, after years and years of Harv "lovin' the ladies," (Leona's daughter's phrase) — Elzina lost her mind. Mama told me about that. She said, "Don't worry about it, I'm sure it's not inherited, but Cleve's mother was in a mental hospital for a year and a half. When she went home the doctor told her, *'Just go home and don't ever pay any attention to Harv again, and you'll be alright.'"*

"*And she did,*" my mother always finished. "*And she was.*"

But losing her mind came later, in mid-life. In 1908 they were living with "Jesus Christ." She was probably already pregnant with a third child, and she was saying "No. I'm going back to my folks."

Mama said "Never tell anyone . . . never, never tell anyone this. I'd be so ashamed. Cleve's mother and father lived in a log cabin with a dirt floor. Never tell anybody that."

"OK, Mama. I won't."

Leona said it, too. "We were awful poor." Flat fact, a kind of sorrow in her voice: "They just had a little log cabin with a dirt floor." She glances at me, then, and I know there has been an instantaneous reading of my face. I don't mind. I, too, learned to read the faces of more affluent people, in those years growing up in two crowded rooms in St. Louis. Later I take count. Eleven people in a log cabin with a dirt floor. No: nine people. Two of the babies had died.

LATER, at home, I will try to catch her voice on the tape I made as she talked. Only fragments will come through over the roar of the little air conditioner in the window of her trailer house. *"Cleve was the only one of us kids that got any schooling you might say at all. He wouldn't stay at home. The rest of the boys had to work. They didn't want to go to school. He really wanted to go to school, so he lived with my aunt and uncle and helped them on the farm down there and got what schooling he got. None of us got much schooling at all."*

She said when he was a young man, my father went up to houses and asked people for something to eat. *"Lester was a year or two younger, and they was going around together. Lester told us that Cleve would go up there and he'd come back with plenty to eat. Lester said, 'Cleve'll stop at anybody's house. I'm not going with him no more.' But Cleve said, 'If you get hungry you will.'"*

My father. How hungry do you have to get before you ask a stranger for food?

Leona said, *"But Cleve was good lookin'."*

1908. Cleve would not be born for another five years; Lester and Leona, later still. Their mother, Elzina, was not yet twenty, but she was saying she was going to take her two babies, and go home to her parents. She

Wake Up Laughing

didn't believe that preacher was Jesus Christ. And she couldn't take it any more.

Under that kind of pressure, Harv went to the preacher, and asked to borrow his horse and wagon so he could take his wife and children to Ava, to her parents. The preacher said "No way. You can find your own way to take them."

Jesus Christ who will never die said, "No. You can't use my horse. You can't borrow my wagon."

Harv waited a couple of days, and then in the middle of the night he stole the horse and wagon. I doubt that he thought he was stealing from Jesus Christ. I suspect he lost his faith in the very moment of the preacher's "*No.*" He loaded up his family under cover of night, and left. They got halfway to Ava before the sheriff caught up with them. Harv was taken off to jail. Nobody knows how Elzina and the babies got home.

Harv was scared to death that they would hang him, so he convinced the other men who were in the jail to help him dig out. They did it; they dug out of the jail, but then the other men got scared and refused to leave. Harv was the only one who ran away. He hid for a long time in a cave, and Elzina's mother took him food and water every day.

When I was a little girl, Mama took me to Brown's Cave, a huge open mouth in the side of a cliff to which there was no road. The opening was so big, a two story house could have sat in it, and nobody knew how long or deep it was. We got there on foot after somebody took us in a jeep over rough fields beside a small river. Perhaps that is the cave where my grandfather hid. My mother would not have told me; she wanted me to forget that there was any family other than hers, and so I had no idea that somewhere there was a grandfather named Harv who sure did love the ladies, and a grandmother named Elzina who had one small snapshot of me standing beside an old car, holding a doll.

After a long time in the cave, Harv went to another town, used a different name, and got a job. *"For years and years he was scared to death he would be caught."* I think of him now, a young man hiding in a cave. Caves are always cold. They are always very dark. He believed they would hang him. *"That's what they did in those days,"* Leona said. *"That's what they did to horse thieves."*

25

FACTS

There were four boys, three girls. In order: Alvin, Marie, Tom, Cleve, Lester, Linnie and Leona. And two babies who died in infancy.

Linnie died at age seventeen, in childbirth.

Lester died at age twenty-four, shot to death by a shotgun through a screendoor.

Tom died of Lou Gehrig's disease at age sixty. Two wives. Many kids.

Marie married several times, had a boy and a girl. An alcoholic, she died in an institution.

Leona married twice. Two daughters, Bernice and Rebecca, and one son.

Cleve died on the operating table during his second operation for ulcers.

Harv's grandparents had come from Holland to Pennsylvania. They never learned to speak English. Harv's parents lived around Ava. Many of Harv's and Elzina's relatives are buried in the Ava cemetery.

Elzina's maiden name was Lakey. Her mother's maiden name was Cotton. Lakey is the Native American name.

Elzina did not smoke. She had three strokes in three years. She had high blood pressure and died of a heart attack at age sixty-nine.

Harv, Elzina and Linnie are buried in the Gasper Ridge Cemetery, on the business route of Highway 44. Leona will be buried there when she dies, next to her second husband. Cleve and Tom are buried in the Waynesville town cemetery.

Leona's daughter Bernice said, "Grandpa (Harv's father) planted pine trees. To this day I wonder what they did with them. Did he sell them for Christmas trees or what? Pine trees all over that farm. They used to have chickens and grandpa would gather up nuts to feed to the chickens. Hickory, walnuts, butternuts."

Harv was married before he married Elzina, to a woman named Alfie, who died. They had a daughter. Leona said Harv and Elzina "moved up to Waynesville (from Ava) about 1936. They lived down on the ridge. We were so poor — a little log cabin with a dirt floor . . . "

I asked Leona what kind of work Harv did, and she said, "Oh, just anything he could get. He worked for farmers . . . Mama was eighteen when they married. That was pretty old then." Harv smoked a little, not a lot. He died of a heart attack in his eighties.

I told Leona that Mama always said Harv had a child by his own retarded daughter. I watched shock move over her face. She took a long drag on her cigarette, then said slowly, looking at the ashtray as she stubbed it out, "*I wonder which one of us she thought was retarded.*"

26

"LESTER had a name for drinkin' and fightin'." Lester was her older brother, one of the two other youngest children who were still at home with Leona as she was growing up in the log cabin with the dirt floor. The older six children were dead or gone away.

"Lester was married. They had a baby. She left him, took the baby over to her folks place. Lester, he went over there and her father was there with a shotgun behind the screen door. Lester couldn't see him there. He walked up on the porch and that old man shot him through the screen door. With a shot gun. Shot him dead. He was only twenty-four years old."

I asked, "What happened? Did the old man go to jail?"

"Five years. It was cold-blooded murder and he got five years. They said Lester was on his property."

I have trouble remembering how our conversation went from that moment. It felt as if Lester's death was the bottom of something. The essence of something.

Leona also said of Lester's brother, my father: "He ran off with Sammy once — he just took the little guy and brought him home. My mother told him to take him back. She told Cleve, 'don't go try to see those children when you're drunk.' He couldn't do nothin' when he was drunk."

"The dead are not dead," the African poet Birago Diop wrote.

> *They are in the fire that is dying,*
> *they are in the grasses that weep,*
> *they are in the whimpering rocks.*

In those two days I walked among my own lost dead. And now they are no longer dead. Lester walks up the steps toward the closed screendoor again and again. My father, young and as drunk as his brother Lester, goes to the house of Mama, who has left him, and steals his baby boy. I see them, Lester and Cleve, as if they were not already wasted before they reached twenty five by alcohol and poverty. As if the story still, even now, might have a different end.

"He couldn't see him there," Leona said. The man behind the screen door. The shotgun. And Leona's mother, Elzina, the grandmother, the one who carried the Indian name, the one who carried Native American blood, she told her son, my father, to take his baby back where he got him. "You can't do anything about those children while you're drunk," she said.

27

THESE are my people, I say to myself, and I mean it. *This is my place.* The throb of grasshoppers in the August sun is a rhythm as familiar as the pulse of my own blood, the taking and releasing of my own breath. The voices of Leona and her daughter, Bernice, the voices in the truck stop where I order biscuits and sausage gravy for breakfast, these voices are the one voice that underlies my own speech, the dialect toward which my pronunciation veers.

My children tease me, ask me to say the word, "milk." I say it in two syllables "mee-yelk." They giggle, punch one another, say to their friends, "See?" And to me, "Say it again!" Until I tell them to "bug off," tell them they don't know how much I've changed: they don't appreciate that I've learned not to say "iggle" for eagle, "warsh and rinch" for wash and rinse. I will not let go of "mee-yelk."

These are my people.

At first, I don't much like my cousin Bernice; and I feel in her stiff politeness an equal reservation about me. Me in my rental Buick, coming from God knows where. Leona is my father's sister, but she is only ten years older than I am. I would guess she gave birth to Bernice before she was twenty, which makes Bernice perhaps only ten years younger than I am.

Bernice meets us in her yard. At the edge of the yard, half a dozen men and boys play ball, wrapped in their exaggerated disinterest. Still, curiosity is tangible, seethes in the air, travels from man to man to boy as the ball travels. Thwack!

It was Leona who wanted me to meet Bernice, although she put it as a question: "Do you want to go out to Bernice's house?"

"If you want me to," I answered. "I'll meet anybody you want me to meet, only I'd rather not meet my father's second family."

I had no desire to meet his other wife, his other girls. His other son. Even the desire to meet my father — to stand at the foot of his grave — seemed thin and fragile, strung entirely on Leona's tone of voice that first time I spoke with her, "Is this *Patsy?* Why, *Hon* . . ."

Leona remembers me before I remember myself, and Leona had said, speaking of her daughter, "Bernice said she'd really like to meet you."

"OK," I had said. "Let's go."

BERNICE is a hard-working woman. Lined up around the living room of her little house were perhaps a hundred stuffed dolls and animals: clowns, rag dolls, bunnies in frilly dresses. She had made them for a craft fair the following Saturday. In boxes, rows of little mice in blue dresses. There was no chair back, no shelf, no corner of wall that did not have a doll or an animal propped against it.

We sat at the kitchen table drinking coffee from mugs. "Did your mother teach you to sew?" I asked, and she replied a little sharply, "No! I taught myself!"

Leona nodded. "That's the truth. She taught herself everything she knows." The tone was genuine acknowledgment. I remembered how, as we sat on her trailer porch, Leona told me about her second husband, to whom she was married for thirty-five years: "He wasn't good to me. He beat me when he was drinking. But then, we both drank."

I am interested in Leona, and moved by her. She is the one who, after her mother died, took care of Harv for years before he died. She is the caretaker in her generation.

Bernice, early in our conversation, expressed bitter anger toward my mother, and Leona nodded agreement. The words were the same words Leona had spoken on her trailer porch earlier, but the expression was much more bitter. "Your mother had *no right* doin' what she done. It wouldn't of hurt you to see your grandma and your grandpa. They loved you. Your mother did an awful thing, keepin' you away from them." I felt Bernice's anger extended to me — and I felt no need to defend myself. That is, until the moment at the end of our visit with Bernice, when we took leave of one another in her yard, hugging each other stiffly, and she told me (a little smugly?) that it sure was too bad I had missed out on so much. Until that moment — and in some sense even *in* that moment — I agreed fully with her assessment of my mother's attitude. It was "an awful thing." And so, when Bernice said so, in her kitchen, I agreed.

I asked Bernice if she liked her grandfather — then stumbled and said "I guess I should say *"our grandfather."* Again, her answer was sharp, reprimanding: "He's *your* grandfather, too!"

She said, moving quickly to the refrigerator to get milk for the coffee — a quick woman, a busy woman, a hard-working woman — "Oh, yes, I loved that old man!" Then, as if it were part of the same statement, "He never saw a woman who wasn't beautiful. He messed around with them even as an old, old man." Laughter. "But he was always cheerful. He was a little Dutchman. Muscular. And grandma, she was so jealous — even when he was so old he couldn't do a thing about it, he loved the ladies, and she was always jealous." She sat back down, lit up a cigarette. "She cried a lot. And he was hard on her." Leona nodded, agreeing. "He always criticized the food she cooked, always had something to say about it that wasn't nice. And she let it get to her — Grandma was too sensitive. He didn't mean no harm by it. Yes, I loved that old man."

I told her Hilda, my father's second wife, and then Leona, had said there was "Indian blood" in Elzina's ancestry. Bernice was emphatic, "Oh, yes. Cherokee. Her grandfather was full-blooded Cherokee." I felt myself doubting. This was Osage country, I thought; the names, the area, the word "Ozark" itself. "It was her grandfather who was full-blooded Indian?" I asked.

"Yes," she said, looking to Leona, who nodded agreement. "There was a picture of that old man. Long hair, braids. Tom had it. When Grandpa died, Tom went in to their log cabin and took everything. I don't know what ever happened to that picture, but I remember it very clearly when I was little. And I remember Grandma talking about him."

I told Bernice, as I had told Leona, that I dreamed Elzina speaking to me, and in the dream she said, "What I have to offer you is Native American."

Bernice looked thoughtful, took a long drag on her cigarette. Then she nodded, said "Grandma believed in things like that. Yeah, that's something Grandma would do." It seemed to me in that moment, for a moment, there was a softening in Bernice's attitude toward me.

Back on her own porch, Leona had also felt comfortable with the idea of her mother speaking in a dream. She said, "Mom believed in 'tokens.' She would have believed in that." Leona said Elzina looked out one night and saw lights on in Lester's car, and told him to go out and turn his lights off. He went out, and came back in, and said, "There weren't any lights on, Mom." The next day, when he was shot dead by his father-in-law, Elzina remembered the lights, and said what she had seen was "a token."

Leona didn't want to stay long at Bernice's. I respect Bernice, the hard work she is doing, the living she and her husband are wresting from that rocky place, the yard in which her boys, her men, play ball. But I was glad Leona didn't want to stay. Bernice was not the reason I made the journey. We looked at each other across a huge divide that was not of our own making. I was ready to go.

28

WHEN we left Bernice's, I asked Leona to take me to the place where Aunt Nellie and Uncle Elmer had their filling station. It was a lot to ask, since that was the place where her family tried to see me, and was repeatedly turned away.

Before we went to Bernice's, we had finished talking on Leona's front porch, sipping coffee while I leaned into my pages of paper, taking notes, asking questions, and keeping a little tape recorder going.

We had finished, too, visiting graves: my father, his brother, his parents, Leona's husband. Beside her husband's grave, a year old and marked only by the rough curve of rocky ground and a tangle of plastic flowers, Leona's face had twisted into grief. *"He wasn't good to me. He beat me — but then, we both drank —"* her voice soft, her words slow. *It's awful hard, being alone."*

I was struck again and again, talking with Leona and Bernice, with how implicitly both of these women accepted the drunkenness, violence and womanizing of men. They *smiled* when they spoke of it — as if they were talking about the misdemeanors of a pet dog or cat. It was, I think, the sea they had always been swimming in. A natural element. A kind of helpless acquiescence, as one sometimes feels watching the brutality of nature — a hawk with a rabbit, a snake with a frog, a spider with a fly —

the agonized scramble, the twitching pitiful legs, the amoral and inexplicable rawness of the way things are. In Bernice, it was in speaking of her grandfather (still I stumble — *my* grandfather) Harv. How he had "loved the women." How he "chased them until he was too old to do a thing . . ." And laughter. How his wife, 'Zina, was jealous. How she "got her feelings hurt real easy."

They didn't talk about her breakdown. Except when I asked Leona if what Mama said was true, that Elzina had a breakdown, she nodded. "Yes." She said. "That's true."

She showed me where the filling station stood. I had said, please just show me; I don't think I can find it by myself. I'll go back there tomorrow morning. She was silent as we drove up the hill. I could sense the old sting, the hurt, in her silence. Beyond that little stretch of old asphalt off Highway 44 (66, in those days) I was hidden from Leona's family, was told to play only *behind* the station, had been offered a keyhole view of my father.

"Lawson's station was right there, I think," she said. That was grace.

We didn't talk about it as we drove past. It was too tangible, too actual, the memory. Ghosts certainly stood in the rooms of my mind: Aunt Nellie bending over her books at the counter of the station, Uncle Elmer talking politics as he pumped gas, Mama's mother dying in the back room, Mama standing beside me as she told me to lean down and look through the keyhole. Leona's ghosts seemed there, too, at the edges of my own memory. Her mother asking to see me. Hearing the answer, "*No*."

There seemed nothing more to say, in fact, about anything. As if we had reached some kind of bottom point in sounding the emotional truth between us.

I reminded her that I had written in letters that I'd like to take her to dinner. "Someplace nice," I said. "After all, this might be once in a lifetime."

Wake Up Laughing

She suggested we go to MacDonalds.

I said, "Leona, I'll take you wherever you'd like to go, but I did want to take you someplace nice."

She said, "MacDonalds is OK."

I left it at that; we would eat at MacDonalds.

Before we left her trailer to go to the graves, she had lifted the sheet strung on a cord across the door to her back room, disappeared and returned in a pretty, silky blue blouse. She is a good-looking woman. I liked knowing as I looked at her that we look a lot alike. I told her so. The blue blouse was lovely on her; she must have been stunningly beautiful when she was a young girl.

On the way to MacDonalds we drove past a Ramada Inn. Leona said in that quiet voice that I was learning to love, "They say there's a nice place to eat in there. I s'pose that would be all right."

I turned immediately into the drive, grateful that she was allowing me to do something special. It was early; only one other couple was eating in the dining room. I asked for the smoking section, and Leona pulled out her cigarettes as she was sitting down. She ordered catfish; I was tempted — catfish is to Missouri what baked beans is to Massachusetts — but I remembered the tasteless job I had done of trying to cook catfish once back home in Massachusetts. Leona suggested, wisely, that I order something else and taste her catfish. We traded bites in the candlelight — my chicken, her fish. The catfish was delicious. She said as we finished, "I'm not nosey — yes I am. How much did this cost?" I showed her the bill; it was less than twenty dollars. She said she thought it would have cost a lot more than that.

29

RETURNING

When you go back
to a place you have loved
and the houses are gone
and the trees that knew you by heart
have vanished,
and earth-moving equipment
has altered even the lay of the land,
don't grieve.
All you have loved whispers to you
in the slightest motion of wild grass,
each thin stalk bearing in its seeds
the weight of the future.

THE filling station is gone; in its place is a cheap honky-tonk nightclub. Where I walked as a child on the old, blacktop road across which the army blasted a precipitous gully fifteen feet deep to prevent traffic by any means but the main gate into Fort Leonard Wood, now there is no road.

Wake Up Laughing

This was the place I mentioned to the psychic that day with Naomi: "Ask him if he will meet me in the cut in the rock," and was given the answer, "He will meet you when you come out of that place."

E A R T H - M O V I N G machines have changed the slope of the hill. On the day that I returned, heat shimmered over the gravely ground, sunlight caught flecks of calcite, flashed signals: *Here. Look here.* They were false messages, or if true, coded in a language I could no longer understand.

Whatever construction had been undertaken, had been abandoned. Or perhaps the whole purpose was the removal of earth for some construction elsewhere. Monolithic hulks of rocky soil remained where telephone poles prohibited earth moving tractors from moving earth. The mounds were shaped a bit like the forbidding towers of nuclear reactors, and each one was topped by a telephone pole. Three of them stood in a line that pointed in the direction of the old road, toward the deep cut I came here to see. They looked to me like absurd monuments.

I was briefly aware of the dialogue with the psychic, but it was thin and watery compared to the weight of memories that met me in that place. Bareheaded in the August heat, I faced the vanished filling station. If Leona had not taken me to this place the night before, I never would have recognized it. The tacky frame building held an oval sign lettered in red: CABARET CLUB. Right. *Cabaret.* A hundred miles from nowhere except dingy little Waynesville on one side and Fort Leonard Wood on the other. Under the building an old concrete slab served as foundation. I surely walked barefooted on that slab in the days when Uncle Elmer bent at its edge to fill a spouted tin can with kerosene, then stuck a potato on the spout to keep it from sloshing out so a kid could carry it home for his parents' lamps. Cracks in the concrete. Ghosts filling ghostly '42 Fords with invisible gasoline from vanished pumps. Inside, Aunt Nellie at the counter, quiet and self-contained like her mother — nothing like her volatile sister, my mother — and behind her row after row of Butterfingers, Baby Ruths, Juicy Fruit gum.

I loved those people, and was loved by them. Until I went away to college, the happiest times of my life were in those hills, as a little child living at Mount Zion and Boiling Springs, and as an older child visiting Aunt Nellie and Uncle Elmer.

NELLIE GRAY

For Nellie Gray Lawson
(b. 1892, d. 1970)

Oh, my darlin' Nellie Gray,
They have taken you away . . .
STEVEN FOSTER

You were the gentle one.
Afternoon and green beans snapping
and the nothing in the Frigidaire
sent you and Uncle Elmer across
Highway 66 walking fast
between the army trucks and drab
civilian cars heading in and out
of Fort Leonard Wood, to the Silver Star
Restaurant and Lounge. Always he
had two eggs over easy and hot milk
sausage gravy on baking powder biscuits.
You had raisin toast and a cup of coffee
and listened while he joked about the Allies
and the Japs. His was the face

Wake Up Laughing

    you presented to the world.
    It was you who minded the cash register
    wrote out the receipts and ordered
    groceries for the station shelves.
    Quiet like your mother, you almost
    disappeared behind his games of checkers
    outside the filling station.
    But I caught you. I still hold you
    after fifty years, the green
    gentle snap of summer beans, the soft
    light of an August afternoon.

I stood in the hot sun and let their faces rise in me. Then I turned my back on the crumbling concrete slab that held the rickety Cabaret Club, and walked toward the place where once there had been an old road into Fort Leonard Wood and a deep cut blasted with dynamite across the road to keep cars from going there.

          • • •

In front of me, wild grass is growing stubbornly on the small spaces around the elevated telephone poles. Tall, thin stalks, their heads heavy with seed, move slightly in air that I cannot feel stirring. The road where I walked was up there, higher than my head. Up there, I walked alone to the cut in the old road, climbed again and again into the earth, an intimate of limestone, lover of fossil, claiming as inestimable gift a chunk of sandstone molded to the shape of prehistoric mud-cracks, treasured finger-tip sized caves full of calcite, its crystals sparkling in that same hot sun. Jewels. There, in the air, was the place I found to go from the war between Mama and my father; her people and — although I didn't know it — his people; from Mama's mother dying; from the incomprehensible sorrows of adults. There I understood for the first time that the earth was my home, fossils were my ancestors. There I named myself child of the curled, prehistoric snail, descendent of the wash of sand into a crack made by sun at the side of a sea lost millennia before my birth. There I understood the ancient Biblical texts: "He hideth my soul in the cleft of the rock . . ." And day after day I came up out of that solitude, drenched with it, protected by it, able to survive.

. . .

WHEN I turned to leave that place, I looked for a moment to see if there was an Indian — a male Indian who knew how to best grow corn. An Indian who, "when I left that place" would "give me my name." I was both amused and disturbed by the absurd image that rose in my mind. An Indian from my childhood — the only Indians I knew: a Walt Disney cartoon — arms folded, lips pursed, saying *"How!"* I was being mocked by my own superstition, by my own generation's ignorance. The blistering heat was making little waves in the air. The sun made my eyes sting. There was no Indian in sight.

30

FOR some reason the tape recorder, which was rendered mostly useless by a noisy little air conditioner in the window of Leona's trailer, caught her voice clearly when she said, "Cleve was the only one of us kids that really got any schooling you might say at all — he really wanted to go to school — he married your mother then . . ."

Later, I would remember the theme: *He wanted schooling. None of us got much schooling at all.* And superimposed on it, Mama's insistence throughout those years in two rooms in St. Louis heat: *Get an education. It is the only way to get out of poverty. Get an education.* How she herself had little formal schooling, and how she feared, above all, that we would not; feared we would be caught, as she had been caught, as our father's family was caught, in poverty. Leona's voice on the tape hesitates, reaches for the images: "I first remember them when they first got married. They bummed a ride on a train — I can barely remember it — we lived in a little town called Cedar Gap. Seymore was the big town up there farther, and your mother and Cleve went to sleep or something and the train went on. They rode right on through Cedar Gap and had to get off and hitchhike back."

MY mother told me about another train trip — to Louisiana, where her father, Richard Ridgway, took her mother, Emma Davis Gray Ridgway, to live in a socialist colony named New Llano, where milk was rationed and given only to the old and the pregnant, and the director was seen stealing his own muskmelons in the moonlight.

On both sides of the family, the grandparents of my generation lived for a while in idealistic communes: Harv and Elzina with a preacher who said he was Jesus Christ; Richard and Emma in a socialist commune. For different reasons — or perhaps not so different — both experiences led to disillusionment.

31

SOUND OF THE NIGHT TRAIN

Only once in every twenty four hours the train comes through my town — in the dark, still center of the night. Sometimes I am awake to hear it wail, a long sound-tunnel back to another time, another place.

1934. Early March in southern Missouri, northern Arkansas. The air cold, the night wind hard in the open doorway of a boxcar headed south toward Louisiana.

My mother told me in the winter of her dying, "I never did tell this to anyone — I was so ashamed. It was the heart of the Depression. We wanted to go to see Papa and Mama in the Socialist Colony down in Louisiana, but we didn't have any money. So we rode the rails. One night a man in the boxcar with us said, 'If you-all know what's good for you, you'll jump right now.' We were scared; we jumped. And me six months pregnant with you. Isn't that awful?"

She lay very still, then, on her high hospital bed, the wedding ring quilt she had pieced when her eyes were good pulled up around her shoulders. What made me sad, listening to this story, was the strangeness of Mama's not saying, "He was just no good." For the first time in her eighty-six years she said, "He was good to me then. I was cold, and we were sleeping on the ground. He covered me with leaves."

She died soon after she told me that story. I listen now sometimes for the sound of the night train, as if that long moan were a tunnel back to that young woman, that young man, in one of the five short years that they were married, and he was good to her, he covered her — covered me — with leaves.

32

I RIDE above clouds and beneath a full moon. The moon flashes reflected light off Lake Michigan, Lake Erie, and a hundred rivers, ponds, little lakes.

Lakes. Lakey. The Native American name, they told me beside those dirt roads, was "Lakey." And I doubted them, wondered if they knew. They had no documents; they had no books. Later, one of my daughters will say, "You can't take this seriously: there is no oral tradition." And I will remember Bernice telling me about the one picture of the grandfather with a single braid down the center of his back, how that picture has disappeared from the hands of one of my father's brothers. I will write a letter and learn that Missouri has no census records in the years that concern my people. And I will think that thin as it is, oral tradition is all I do have.

Between the moon above me and the silver ribbons of rivers below me, I am carried by the steel shell of an airplane. I look down and remember how I walked in the cemetery at Ava, where both my mother's and my father's people are buried. How I stood beside the grave of Emma Ridgway, my mother's mother, and relived her dying and her burial in my thirteenth summer, summer of first blood, of Aunt Nellie's keyhole, of silence on a Greyhound bus. How I stood in front of the tombstone of Aunt Nellie and Uncle Elmer, and grieved for her — wept deeply for her — touching again her quietness, trusting again her love.

As I pulled out of the cemetery in my car, out of the corner of my eye I caught a name on a tombstone — what was it? Ten, twenty miles down the road I thought I heard it in my conscious mind: "Cloud." Was it *cloud*? Cloud Lakey?

It is a measure, I suppose, of my own tippy balance between rationality and whatever is its opposite, that the possibility of an ancestor named "Cloud" convinced me that the Lakeys were indeed Native American. In that ugly, bare, rocky cemetery among these plain Midwestern names: Nellie, Elmer, Emma. *Cloud?*

I wondered if Cloud Lakey was a man or a woman. I wondered, if Cloud was a man, whether he knew when to plant the corn so it would grow. *"When you leave that place, he will tell you your name."* It suddenly occurred to me that "leaving that place" could be interpreted to mean not leaving the cut in the rock, but leaving Missouri. And that the moment, after all, when I turned to leave the cemetery at Ava was the moment when I had seen everything I came to see and turned to leave Missouri. In that moment, in that very last moment, my eye caught the name on the tombstone: Cloud Lakey. Not my individual name, but "Lakey," the name that connected me to my ancestors.

I had a momentary sense of someone, somewhere, laughing.

I want to blame that moment on the moon.

Later, I would learn more about that Lakey tombstone. And I would laugh at myself.

33

Why did we leave the church, Peter?
All that love, all that love
and longing and listening
— do you remember how your hand,
wet with baptismal water,
cupped the head of a baby?
Do you remember putting the little square of bread
carefully on my tongue?
I remember kneeling, I remember
your voice rich and soft in the sanctuary
repeating and repeating the ancient words:
Do this in remembrance of me . . .

AS I began to work on this chapter, I asked Peter to write his thoughts on leaving the church. He wrote pages, and then reduced it to one sentence: "In spite of my effort to forge a relevant ministry, my feeling grew that the church hierarchy and organized religion has no place for someone like me."

I, too, tried to write about our twenty-five years in the ministry, and came to a decision close to Peter's. We loved the people of our local church; we loved our work. We didn't want to leave the vocation to which we felt called, but our understanding of what the church should be was not the same as the understanding held by some members of the hierarchy who unfortunately happened to have control over our lives in the church. We came to feel that we had no choice but to leave or compromise our own vocational integrity.

The prospect of leaving was terrifying. Peter was fifty; I was forty-seven. Our only financial resource was one-fifth of the sale value of one remaining portion of his parents' farm. He estimated our share might be worth about five thousand dollars, if we were lucky, and if it would sell. He asked his sister, who was handling the estate. She said the land had been on the market for years without a single nibble.

Enter Susan DaCosta.

Mrs. DaCosta was a matriarch of the African Methodist Episcopal Zion (AME Zion) Church of Amherst. She and I had become friends early in our Amherst years, because it hurt my heart that a hundred years after the Civil War there was still a white Methodist Church and a black Methodist Church in one little Northern town. I had approached "Mrs. D" as everyone called her, and had asked her if her congregation and our congregation might do an annual Easter sunrise service together. She agreed, and the two of us planned and led it, year after year. A sunrise service at her church, followed by a pancake breakfast at ours.

Mrs. D was a big woman. It was early November of our last year at Wesley church when she called me on the telephone.

"Miz Snyder?" (She never would pronounce the German "Schneider.")

Wake Up Laughing

"Yes. Mrs. D?"

"Could you come over here this morning? Have a cup of tea with me? Right now?"

"Well . . . sure."

"Come right now. And don't bring anybody with you. Hear?"

"OK"

I was intrigued by her tone; I felt myself *summoned*. Which, it turned out, was an absolutely correct assumption.

Mrs. D lived on a quiet, tree-lined street about three blocks from Wesley. It was an old farmhouse with a front porch, the original clapboards covered with asbestos shingles for insulation. She welcomed me at the door and took me in to her dining room where the table was covered by a lace tablecloth. And she told me the story of her life.

She was married as a young woman to Mr. Jones, who was a part-time pastor of the AME Zion Church. Ever after, regardless of his death and several subsequent marriages, she thought of herself as a minister's wife, and took her responsibilities at the little church near Amherst College campus with great seriousness.

In the middle of the depression of the 1930's, times were hard for the little church, and Mr. Jones became discouraged. He wanted to leave the church.

This was the first indication I had that Mrs. D knew what was going on in my life. She looked at me meaningfully, measuring my expression. "He was discouraged because we didn't have enough money to live on, but I told him, 'Don't leave. I'll pray.' And I did," she said. "And after I got through praying, I got up off my knees and I called the district superintendent and I told him we don't have enough money out here to run this little church. And the next annual conference, they voted more money for us."

I nodded; we grinned at one another. I understood that kind of praying — it was the way of prayer for her generation of wives. I had tried it, too. I had spoken privately to our district superintendent. He told me I had a problem with authority.

She measured me in her powerful gaze and tipped the teapot to refill my cup. "A few years later, he got discouraged again. He said, 'We have to leave. We aren't going to make it, we have to leave.' I told him to wait until after annual conference. He was in an accident on the way home from that conference. He died instantly."

I started to express my sorrow to hear that, but she held up her hand for me to wait for the rest of her story. She was living with their one son in a little apartment above the drug store in the center of Amherst. Things were very, very hard. One night she dreamed that an old lady named Miz Jenkins came to her door and knocked. When Mrs. D opened the door, Miz Jenkins held out her hand and said, "Here is the key."

The dream troubled Mrs. D. She felt it was a message, but she couldn't figure it out. She prayed about it, but no understanding came. Several days went by, and then there came a knock at her door. When she opened it, Miz Jenkins stood before her. "I'm too old to take care of my house any more," Miz Jenkins said. "If you will come and take care of me until I die, you and your boy can live with me free."

Mrs. D said, "This house. I came here to this house, and I took care of Miz Jenkins, and when she died, she willed this house to me. I have lived here for forty-two years. I raised chickens in the back yard and took care of white folks when they had new babies or when they were sick."

She looked at me with as intense a gaze as I have ever experienced. "You like this house?" she asked.

I felt confused and — I admit it — a little frightened. A nod seemed appropriate.

She sighed then, and pulled herself painfully up onto her feet. "Come here," she said, and led the way into her living room where she settled

Wake Up Laughing

into an easy chair and motioned me to the couch, under a lighted picture of John and Robert Kennedy on either side of Martin Luther King.

"I went to the ecumenical service at St. Bridgets yesterday," she said. "I was sitting there after the service was over, just sitting there for a while, and all at once God spoke to me. He said, you sell that house to the 'Snyders.' That's what He said." Her voice became gentle and soft, and I believe she said what she had been rehearsing for years. "Now I'm too old to take care of this house. I can't go up and down stairs any more. I've been renting to students for years, but I can't provide for them any more. If you want it, you can buy it."

"Mrs. D," I said. "Thank you with all my heart, but it's not possible. We don't have any money at all. We've always lived in a furnished parsonage. We don't even have any furniture. We still owe $5,000 in student loans from our college days. We drive an old car that is almost broken down, and we have four kids. We can't buy a house!"

"What are you going to do?" she asked, and I realized that she knew almost as much about us as we knew about ourselves.

"I don't have any idea," I said.

"Never mind!" Her voice rang out. "Never mind! God makes a way out of no way!" And again, the commanding tone: "Let us pray."

Mrs. D's prayers rocked the universe. They were filled with little exclamations of joy, little gasps of ecstasy. They cajoled, praised, caressed the divine presence. I had heard her pray before. She was a mighty woman. This time, when she finished praying, she dismissed me from her presence as if the deal were done.

MEANWHILE, our grief over leaving our community, our lifetime work, and our essential orientation, mounted. We were told by the bishop and his cabinet that our work was creative, but it wasn't "Methodist" enough. The fact that our people loved us was interpreted by one member of the cabinet as dangerous. Perhaps, he suggested, we were headed toward another "Jonestown." The bishop asked Peter to stay in the ministry and accept another appointment. Ten years was considered a long pastorate — we had been in one parish for fifteen years. The appointment he suggested offered a raise in salary, but had nothing whatever to do with the work we had been doing, or to which we felt called.

A friend of Peter's, another Methodist minister, suggested to him that he request early retirement. "After all," the friend said, "you have given twenty-five years of distinguished service."

AND there you are, Peter, a young man. Your hair so black, so thick, your farmer's hands strong from summers on the tractor and in the barn. I am back in the pew with your mother and your father; you are up in front. We have sung glorious hymns — words set to Beethoven's "Hymn to Joy":

> *Joyful, joyful we adore Thee,*
> *God of Glory, Lord of love,*
> *Hearts unfold like flowers before Thee,*
> *Opening to the sun above . . .*

• • •

The bishop and the district superintendents and your home town pastor surround you as you kneel. They all lay their hands on your head. They pray for you. They confirm the ordination that they say is from God.

• • •

Peter requested early retirement.
The answer came quickly: "No."

Wake Up Laughing

OUR only remaining option was to take our retirement money out of the general retirement fund. The church conference put two dollars into the fund for every one dollar contributed by the pastor. If you took out your money before full retirement, you forfeited the church's portion. After twenty-five years, we had contributed eight thousand dollars to the retirement fund. Taking it out would mean forfeiting their sixteen thousand — a hugely frightening prospect, in our circumstances.

Peter wrote the letter asking for the eight thousand dollars. He received a letter in response. We never inquired whether it represented church polity at that time, or only the action of one individual, but it was simply unbelievable to me: If you want your eight thousand dollars, the letter said, you will have to mail in your ordination.

• • •

He's the lily of the valley, the bright and morning star . . . I never can remember the lines that follow. I believe that the church is a place where many people touch the mystery at the heart of life, and I believe it is a place where many people turn and do good work to heal the brokenness of the world. I still believe that, today, as I write these words. The most painful thing about any divorce is not the hateful things that happen, but the love. The love that will not let you go. The love that keeps on, and keeps on, bringing back fragments of the old songs.

• • •

PETER mailed in his ordination, and we left. When all our bridges were burned, and there was no place for us to go — at what seemed the last possible moment, Peter's sister called. The final piece of property from their parents' farm had sold. Peter's share was $20,000. We tithed $2,000, bought a new car for $8,000 and put $10,000 down payment on Mrs. D's house at 77 McClellan Street, Amherst. We have been here now for sixteen years. I hold her house in trust. I care for her lilacs, I watch snow pile up on the branches of her pine tree. Each spring, I lift to my face the perfect perfume of her lilies of the valley. When I walk barefoot across her old wood floors, I can feel her footprints, there before me.

34

AFTER my trip to Missouri, the year rolled around to another June, and it was time to go to lead my workshop in Ireland again. By this time I understood that whatever else these journeys to Missouri and Ireland were about, they were about healing my spiritual life.

In some deep sense, my own writing and the free writing workshops I had led for low income women over the preceding ten years enabled me to work with remembered images and gave me the context in which to heal my childhood. What remained was that I needed to complete the healing of my spirit.

Part of that work lay ahead of me in continuing to write. I needed to work with images of the new discoveries I had made in Missouri, to come to understand what they could teach me.

Another part of the work of healing lay in Ireland, and I decided to be open to the possibility of receiving that gift. Even more, I decided to actively invite the fullness of spiritual healing to happen.

How does one do that, when one has lost a vocabulary of religious experience? When the familiar language of spiritual life simply doesn't work any more? Well, I don't know. I guess by turning one's face toward the unknown, and saying "I know you have been calling my name. I am answering. And the answer is 'Yes.'"

It makes me very angry to think of Máire as unqualified by her church for its priesthood. Whether or not she might wish for that confirmation, it angers me profoundly that it would not be available to her. From the moment she spoke my name on the campus of Pacific School of Religion until this moment as I write, Máire has acted toward me with dignity and with warmth; she has brought me compassion and challenge and an unspoken insistence upon my spiritual growth even when I was dead-set against climbing the iron fences to where it moved among wild grasses and nettles.

Even though I had disavowed any need for a priest, it was in a real sense to my priest, therefore, that I wrote what for me was quite a vulnerable request. It was the first act in preparing myself for the third summer in Ireland as a conscious welcoming of spiritual healing. I told her I would like — if it was possible to purchase such a thing in an antique shop or somewhere (and if for some religious reason the request was inappropriate, please disregard it and remember my ignorance) — I would like her to find for me an old rosary. If possible, one which had belonged to a Sister.

I cannot imagine in my wildest fantasy that I will ever embrace any organized church again. I don't know why I wanted a rosary. But I did. And I told her I didn't want a new one; I wanted one that had been held in a woman's hands, and used. I wanted the sense of the spirit of the woman lingering in the beads, meeting my own spirit. Máire knew that I do not know how to pray a rosary. I knew that she knew. It was an act of trust on my part to ask her this favor. She did not ever mention the request to me, in any letter or telephone conversation. This from a correspondent who reads my letters and responds line by line. Consistently. I was aware of her silence, but I knew she had heard the request. I trusted her, and did not feel uneasy about it. I even imagined the possibility that the request was in fact inappropriate; perhaps we would never mention it again. And even that felt all right, because she had been with me in the church at Dún Lúiche, and in the cemetery at Moat. She would not doubt the spirit of my request.

After writing the letter asking for the rosary, I walked six miles along the edge of the surf on Block Island, where I was spending a few days writing. I thought about women throughout history, trying to understand their own spiritual lives in a context in which most of the institutions are led by, created by, controlled by men. I thought about my daughters; I have three, and a daughter-in-law whom I love as a daughter. And my son. I have one. I thought about my granddaughter and my grandson. Then I thought about my mother, how poor her parents were, how she married in the midst of the Great Depression because they couldn't afford to feed her, how she wanted education, how they struggled with religion. I thought about rosaries, and how I do not know how to pray a rosary, and do not even have a desire to learn.

As I walked back toward the hotel — a little slowly because I was tired, and because the sandpipers were so magical at the edge of the water, and the beached baby starfish needed throwing back into the sea, and there were such treasures in the sand: shiny stones, bits of polished glass — I picked up a broken shell, the inner spine exposed, the inner surface smooth, pink, ivory, and found the rhythm of my walking falling into a very old Protestant hymn. It was the only one my mother knew how to play on the piano, and so I heard it played simply, a little shyly, the few times when she felt comfortable to touch a piano in someone else's house. And I heard her sing it sometimes, to herself. I don't think of it as good theology. I didn't make a conscious choice that day to sing that song. Suddenly I just noticed, as I was walking, that I had been singing, out loud, over and over as the waves crashed in and fell back to the Atlantic. I must have sung the only sentence of that song that I remember fifty or sixty times, thinking about other things as I was singing. *Out of the ivory palaces/into the world of woe/only his great, eternal love/made my Savior go.*

Pat Schneider

When I became aware of myself singing, I paid attention to the words, thought about what they mean, and remembered that when I was young I believed their meaning literally. I wondered whether, now, in any metaphoric sense, I do still believe them. Wondered, is it true, did *the holy one* actually enter human history as a specific human person? And if so, only once? Only as a man? And who is Jesus to me now? And what is the holiness of the five-thousand-year-old images carved in the stone of the passage grave at Newgrange? The triple spirals, turning in and in, out and out, without end.

IT felt to me that I was "doing theology," all day as I walked. As I wrote. As I sang the strange old words my mother sang: *Out of the ivory palaces, into the world of woe* . . .

Virginia Woolf, in *A Room of One's Own,* wrote, "We think back through our mothers, if we are women." It occurred to me that maybe we Protestant women sing old hymns the way Catholic women say their rosaries. The repeated and repeated words, rising from deep memory to the lips. In my tradition, moving on melody. In Máire's tradition, moving on beads.

I KNEW that I wanted a rosary, and was, by requesting one, opening myself somewhat to the tradition of women in the Catholic church. The second thing I knew was that I wanted to go back to Newgrange and to the church at Dún Lúiche, and that in each of those places which felt holy to me, I would consciously open my mind to the possibility of the healing of my spirit.

I didn't know what that healing would look like, or feel like, but I did know I had had enough of grief. I had had enough of the anger that doesn't take you anywhere except deeper and deeper into your own rut. I felt I had learned a lot by returning to Pacific School of Religion twice a

Wake Up Laughing

year to lead workshops, and each time writing honestly out of the truth of my own life, out of the discoveries each new year brought. And I learned and grew in the first two years in Ireland. But I still was a person *in reaction* to things I had turned from, rather than a person healed of the past and open to the future, healthily growing spiritually.

That third June in Ireland, Máire and I planned a week together in addition to the week of the workshop, but I arrived with a partially healed broken arm, a heavy cold, and an exhaustion that very nearly spoiled our vacation.

Near the end of that week, Máire said gently that she was going to Mass, and invited me to go with her if I wanted to. I had not gone to Mass since that first, painful experience. I said yes, I did want to go. Then she told me she had a rosary for me; in fact, she had "sent out word," to four Mother Superiors (!!!!), told them for whom the rosary was intended, and that it must be very special. Before she gave it to me she said that it is old; each bead is hand-carved of green marble; it belonged to an Irish Sister in Africa; and she said very quietly, and I think a little vulnerably, that she thought this one, of others she might have chosen, was right for me because the figure of Christ was broken off the cross. Only one tiny foot remained, attached to one tiny nail.

She put the rosary into my hands. What she did not know was how intensely personal the design of the cross was for me: over the front of it there is a delicate tracery of lily of the valley.

With my rosary hidden in my hand in my pocket, we went to Mass, perhaps both of us with some trepidation, remembering the experience of Mass my first year in Ireland. We were in Donegal; the liturgy turned out to be in Irish. Máire was delighted; I was delighted. She loved hearing and understanding in Irish; I loved hearing and *not* understanding liturgy with which I would probably have internally argued. The priest was a dear young man who spoke his homily in English, telling of being on the sea in his father's boat in a storm. When it came time for the Eucharist, Máire whispered to me: "I just want you to know you are welcome, if you want to come with me."

It was clear to me that the invitation was from Máire, not from the priest. I was this time not seduced into any false welcome. I knew perfectly well that the priest knew I was not Catholic. It was a small country church. He gave several warm welcomes to visitors, looking, I thought, in my direction, and I knew not a single word of liturgy nor did I properly bow before entering the pew, etc. etc. I knew he knew who I was. Nevertheless, *my* priest had invited me, and I wanted to receive communion for the first time in many years. So I followed Máire out of the pew. When she had received, and moved on, I was face to face with the priest. He had been putting the wafers into cupped hands; I cupped my hands. He looked me in the eye with one of the straightest, unsmiling looks I have ever received, and with great precision placed the wafer in my hands. I looked back at him with the straightest, unsmiling look I had in me, and with great precision put the wafer on my tongue. It was a moment of intense communication; I am absolutely certain of it. His look was not unfriendly, but it was intensely serious. I *felt* him say to me, "I know what you are doing." I felt myself saying to him, "I know what I am doing." I felt he gave me, knowing I was not a Catholic, what to him was the Body of Christ. I felt I took what to me was a step toward saying *yes* to the healing of my own spirit, in my own way, in my own time.

I was so absorbed in my memories of communion, I sat expecting the "ushers" to bring around the cup, and was stunned to realize the Mass was over. A little disoriented, I saw that only the priest and the local Sisters received the cup. I had expected this, but had slipped momentarily into my own past, lost between the cracks of our two traditions.

Poor Máire, who had shepherded me so gently, was relieved to know the experience of Mass for me had been solid and good; the encounter with the priest moving and honest.

Wake Up Laughing

I sensed that I would probably never take communion again, and this time that awareness was one of beginning, not of ending.

SHE took me to the two places I wanted to revisit. Dún Lúiche still clung to the foot of the mountain, and the broken church was still magical, beautiful, but I knew when we arrived there that I had already received the gift it had held for me. What had happened there had already happened. There is a sign near the gate that amuses me. It is hanging on the fence which is intended (not very successfully) to keep sheep out. The sign says CONSECRATED GROUND. NO CAMPING. Whatever it was that I was seeking this year, it was not to be given me at my beloved Dún Lúiche church. And Newgrange was a similar experience; it was perfectly wonderful, but safely back in its own history and mystery.

AT last we traveled to Sligo to St. Angela's College for the workshop — the deepest, truest, best workshop I had up to that time ever led. Máire opened each of the five days with a story about Jesus and a woman.

Near the end of the workshop, the story we considered was the one in which Jesus goes to the bedside of the little girl who has died, and says to her, *"Talitha, kumi," (Little girl, I say to you, arise).* This phrase in the text is particularly moving, because it is one of three statements by Jesus that has been preserved in his own native tongue, Aramaic. On that day, I realized that in leading the workshop with seventeen participants, I myself had not actually written anything that was new to me.

I had written things I have written before, stories that were new to the women who heard me read them, but they were not truly risky for me. I have always believed that in my teaching it is not fair to evoke other people's risk-taking and take none of my own. I have always written out at the point of risk in the workshops I lead — not necessarily autobiography, but in some sense writing *at the edge of what I understand* — and I determined to do so that day.

I wrote about the secrets of my heart — about my own deepest struggles. I wanted the women in the workshop to see me as I have been, as I am: a complicated human being in whom everything is not resolved, not free of contradiction. I also wrote, in the last session of the workshop, images that were an attempt to get closer to the bed on which I slept as an early teenager when I came home from the orphanage: a bed dirty, sweaty — the journal entry that appears earlier in these pages. I wrote those words under the safety and in the permission of the words, *"Talitha, kumi."*

THE workshop ended on Friday, and my flight was on Monday. We did some shopping in Sligo, gifts for me to take home to my family, and then stopped on Wine Street outside the shop of Michael, the woodcarver. Both preceding years, Máire suggested I go in and meet Michael. Both years, I resisted, successfully. I'm not sure why, except that his work looked very expensive and wonderful, and I felt a little shy. The first year, Máire said to me, "You should meet Michael." The second year, she went into his shop, and I lingered outside looking at his work in the window. *This* year (behold again the meek nun at work when she thinks something is for my own good which I don't particularly want!!), she went into the shop, spoke to Michael, leaned out the doorway, crooked her index finger in my direction in the imperative mode, kept her eye on me until I stepped in and was introduced to Michael, and promptly announced to me that I was to *stay there and talk to Michael* while she went and put a coin in the parking meter. She disappeared. And was gone a bloody long time, too!

I have to admit that I found Michael fascinating. In the time she was gone he gave me what felt like an introductory course in Irish mythology, Jungian archetypes, Yeats' system of symbols, Joycean imagery, and some kind of magical or holy wisdom, as he turned in his hands a wooden figure I had pointed to in the window, showing me a face, another face, a curved line descending down one side of the body: *"This is the serpent, this is the salmon, this is light and this is dark, this is the animus and this is the anima, this is, and this is, and this is . . ."*

WE left Sligo, and went to Galway, to the home of Máire's sister, Bríd, who was away on vacation. On Sunday morning Máire went to Mass and to visit her mother; I stayed at Bríd's to write in my journal.

This was my last day in Ireland. I had come asking to be released from the grief and anger of my own religious past. I wanted to be set free, and I had asked.

JUNE 1992   In Bríd and Tom Nestor's house, Galway. Máire is (after Mass) at her mother's house.

I woke last night laughing. It was embarrassing, because it waked Máire from her sleep in the single bed opposite me — and we had only moments before, it seemed, finished a deep conversation which acknowledged the end of our days together, and the year that will pass before we will be face to face again. It was a truly sad conversation. And I woke up laughing out loud.

I can't remember what was funny, but I do remember the delicious ripple of the sound, and my own waking sense that "yes, it is as funny as I thought it was — I must remember — I should get up and write it down . . ." And some sense of my children, and some sense of the sound of the laughter of my youngest daughter, Bethany, who has the loveliest laugh in the world.

Pat Schneider

Thinking of it now, I am filled with laughter again — deep inside, where it cannot bubble up to the surface, but effervesces (is there such a word?) in the dark, beneath articulation, as wine must do, in the making, in a dark cellar — bright suns of summer's dandelions making ready to rise under the cork, under the floor of daily life, in the root-vegetable/wine cellar of the unconscious.

Yesterday was hours of talking with Máire, while a fine, Irish rain came in off the Atlantic. We were grateful for the rain, because sun would have called us out to dolmans, sheep, landscapes of external history, and we needed to walk through rooms of inner history.

I think I go home happy. I think a kind of divine humor touched me in the night. The same sense of musical laughter that woke me once years ago on a silent retreat and I thought it was angels — and again here, last night, only this time it is my own laughter — but too beautiful, laughter beautiful beyond what my body could make — the feeling of it lingering in my own dark depths, like the spots and streaks of light Máire and I collected in dark rocks on Sligo beach: ancient fossils, crinoid stems, looking like stars falling through a black sky, caught in stone for three million years — laughter like that, timeless, in motion, motionless. And now, as I write, suddenly there is a stillness in my mind, an absolute silence, in which I see the face of God! — I see the face of God — why not? Why not? Who was it who ever said a mortal may not look on the face of God and live? How did he know?

I am sitting in this ordinary chair in this kitchen of Bríd, while Máire sits talking with their mother after a Mass I chose not to attend. I see the face of God and there is laughter behind the eyes and behind the grin (not smile, grin) and it is only one face of God who has many faces like the statue in the window of Michael

Wake Up Laughing

Quirke the woodcarver of Sligo who was a butcher and carved wood and three years ago gave up butchering and carves and talks poetry and Irish mythology behind the window of his shop on Wine Street.

I am stunned by the color of a blossom in an earthenware pot on the counter of this kitchen. The blossom red against the earth pot against the white wall. I want to write a book straight through without looking back. I want to remember what I have forgotten if it comes to me, as it comes to me, and let it go if it does not come of its own free will, like a cat comes, silently, with an air of independence — a cat that roams freely at night, choosing its own times of wildness among the tall grasses, the borders of wilderness at the edges of our small cultivations — and its own times of tame companionship, purr of pure pleasure, sun on the common windowsill, red blossom, earth pot, painted wall. I want to write like that cat lives.

What I forgot to say about the face of God was what surprised me most — not that the face was laughing, but that the face was a woman's face. And that beyond the woman's face, turned away, with just an edge of cheekline visible, another face looked toward shadow — not threatening, not problematic — a man's face. And I knew there was at least one more face, completely unseen, on the dark side of the moon/the head/the figure/the statue in the hand of the woodcarver Michael standing in the butcher shop turned carver shop — this world — Sligo . . . Another face which I could not see. All three faces moved me deeply, but it was the woman's face that was in the light, meeting me directly, and her laughter was ocean and all waters, and deep beyond what my ears could hear. Deeper. What my bones could feel. Rocked by it, rocked in it.

Oh my God, I remember that I asked. I remember that I prayed: let this trip be about my spiritual journey. I remember, I said I will go to Newgrange again and touch the prehistoric spirals carved in the rock; I will go to the broken church in Dún Lúiche again. Meet me there. I — ex-Protestant, unchurched — asked for a rosary, which was to say, I connect myself to the history of women praying. I went to Mass, which was to say, I remember that I asked and I'm still asking. I went to Dún Lúiche and asked Máire to let me be in that broken church alone. I was saying, I remember that I asked, and I'm still asking.

I will write a book of my days, and I will call it, *Wake Up Laughing*. And these are stories I will want to tell in the book. That I asked.

The answer is here. Now. In this white, ordinary kitchen. In this silence. And the answer is *laughter*. For the first time, the word which rises is "goddess," but it doesn't matter. One face of God is a woman's face, and the face is laughing, and it is one of at least three faces and they are faces that are carved by the hands of a man — no — they are not carved by the hands of any man or woman. And yet they are. Michael, the woodcarver, in the window of the world, carving with his knife. Myself, in the kitchen of the world, carving with my pen. A single peach on a worn-out tree; a round, green, child's marble softened by waves that I found on a beach once when my heart was hurting, and took the marble as a sign; the sound of gentle laughter in the silence of a retreat once, long ago.

Everything a sign. I have seen one of the faces of God and it is a woman's face and it is a form I can hold, no — not hold — a form to make visible to me, this: *laughter*. Beautiful, unspeakably beautiful, laughter.

It is time for Máire to return. We will vacuum the floors, make a lunch, travel to her home in the Dublin convent. Then I will fly to my home. She will appear any moment, because the silence that was being protected is gone. And that is alright. There are tasks to be done. There is the memory of what just happened.

Moments later: Just moments have passed. Máire has entered this kitchen. Her face is warm and tender from her time with her mother, her sister Eibhlín, Eibhlín's Michael, and their unborn baby. I say, "Máire, I want to read to you what I have just written in my journal." And I read to her the words I had written before she came in.

Máire listens. I finish reading. For a while we are silent. And then she says quietly, "Pat, the scripture at Mass today — therefore in churches all over the world — was *'Talitha, kumi.'*"

THAT ecstatic moment has moved back now into gentler eddies at the edges of memory. Like the child's marble at the edge of the ocean, it is not an answer, but an opening. Not an end, but another beginning.

A person's life, like the earth, has its seasons; its griefs and moments of ecstasy are openings into new depths of understanding. Ironically, my own journey has taken me closer to, rather than away from, the teachings of the ancient Hebrew poets and prophets. They knew, after all, that no one can utter the name of God. My work among the poor in the housing projects of Western Massachusetts, I believe, has taken me closer to, rather than away from, the teaching of that radical lover, Jesus.

It is not that the ancient teachers have become less, but that the rest of the universe has become more infused with mystery and grace. Most of our attempts to make religious systems out of the strange intuitions of the human spirit turn out to bind our souls as violently as the feet of women were bound for generations in China. We hobble, spiritually, when we were meant to run and leap and stand solidly in the balance of our souls' maturity.

We are, each one of us, infinitely loved. Our happiness is longed for. We are each seen and known and called by name. That we are set loose in a wild world where nature, cruelty and accident can injure us does not mean that we are not loved, or that we are of no value.

When my children were infants, an older woman friend advised me to keep them in the playpen until they were four years old. I could not do that. Even though they would have been saved bumps and scratches — perhaps my four-year-old daughter would not have lost the sight in one eye — I had to let them walk away from me in a dangerous world. I tried to keep them company for as long as they would allow me to do so. If I did not set them free, they would not become themselves.

We are set free in a dangerous world. But we are not alone in it. We are each held in a most gracious and loving personal attention. It breathes through this natural world and in our dreams and in our visions. It calls us to respond with love for all living things, to compassion and to work for a world where none of us is alone, none of is lost.

CONFESSION

Apprehended on the slant
of air between two trees
crow-fractured morning
after morning, I would
name you if I knew how.
I don't. Know. How
you leap over naming,
sidle under, squeeze around,

Wake Up Laughing

you lilac, thistle, burr,
belonging to no species,
you chipmunk-sudden,
slug-utterly unaccommodating —
you rainfall prism beautiful,
earthquake terrifying,
still of night-deep darkness
comforting,
you rock, you rock,
you unnameable, unknowable known
how you scamper/swim
creep/crawl soar/sink
stride/fly — you mountain, you
desert, delicious, delirious
madness-making laughter
you ocean, you faucet, you ripple,
erupt! Spray! Spout, you silence,
you suggestion, you
impossible, unbelievable
god

35

RECENTLY I dreamed again the house I lived in as a teenager on Olive Street in St. Louis. This time, the dream was different.

Dreams of that house began when I started to write about my childhood. Some of those pieces went into my journal, and became chapters and poems in this book. There were often animals in the dreams, always in danger or deformed. Once there was a man with no head.

After almost fifteen years of this kind of work, the dreams began to change.

In the first changed dream, the house on Olive Street was on fire. Great, roaring flames rose above the building and licked out of the windows. In the dream, I was glad it was burning. It was a cleansing fire. Like Moses' bush, the house was not consumed; the burning would go on forever. It would not burn down, but it would never be the same again. I woke with a feeling that something had fundamentally changed.

The next dream occurred a year or more later. I was in the house, but it had been cleaned. The rooms were still old and in the same configuration, but larger. The wood was still dark and the house was a place where low-income people lived, but it was no longer filthy. I was surprised at the change. I felt deeply ambivalent — both fear and relief, but fear was predominant.

Wake Up Laughing

And then, the final dream. Again I was in the house, but this time it had been completely remodeled. There was an almost festive air to the place, as there is when an old factory has been made into a modern mall of fascinating little shops. It was not a mall; there were still apartments, but they were in no way oppressive. There were clean windows, space, and an honoring of what was old. The most surprising image was the first floor hallway. Where there had been a narrow, dark passage back to the door of the old woman who yelled "Nigger! nigger!" at her twelve-year-old granddaughter, now there was a wide area with an inlaid brick floor — clean and inviting. And behind the stair was a booth with glass windows, and standing in the doorway of the booth was a uniformed police woman. She was doing her work, looking at a piece of paper, but the place was safe and guarded, clean and pleasant.

It is gone, the house that hurt me. It is gone from the earth. In its place in my waking mind, wild blue cornflowers will forever stand, because I don't want to see it with whatever the city builds there. I want to see it covered with a mist of blue flowers, and so I will not ever go back there again. The house in my dreaming mind has been burned into cleanness, redecorated and reclaimed by a new cast of characters whom I do not know. They have my blessing — I am glad they live in a place well lighted, well guarded, where they do not have to be afraid.

36

SOME time after my trip to Missouri, two of my daughters were home for a short visit, and Peter and I took them to Bertucci's, a local pizza place, for dinner. We laughed, enjoyed the sun-dried tomatoes and olives our daughters wanted on the pizza, the mushrooms and green peppers we had chosen. There was a single slice left on the round tin sheet, and we lingered, talking.

We had almost finished eating when something was said about the postcards I had mailed to my four children from the airport in St. Louis as I waited for my flight back to Massachusetts. I don't remember what caused her to remember, but Rebecca said something like, "I couldn't believe you would send me that postcard!"

And I answered, "What postcard?" being at that moment truly ignorant of having caused offense.

"That postcard with a Native American woman on it! I just can't believe you'd do that. You've read papers I've written — you know how I feel, and you sent me that nostalgic photograph of a Native American woman!" She was teaching at Yale, and had published a paper drawing on her dreamlike encounter with Elzina Lakey; she took the matter very seriously, as did her two sisters, one studying feminist theology, the other studying early American literature. All three were working with a particular emphasis on issues of race and gender.

The photographs were beautiful to me. One was dated 1904, the year my mother was born. Another was of a teepee in snow, under tall winter trees. The door to the teepee was open, and a woman stood with her back to the camera, a large bundle of sticks tied below her shoulders. The silence, the seeming privacy of the woman, the sheltering trees were seductive. It was as if I were in the scene, intimately in the scene.

Immediately, as my daughter spoke, I felt I knew what she was saying to me. The very feeling of intimacy in that forest scene is available to me only through the lens of the camera, held in the hands of a white man who is showing me what he wants me to see. The presence of the white viewer is invisible in the photograph, and I am invisible as I look into the life of that woman. There is a trespass in the feeling of intimacy. The open door of the teepee is not open to welcome me, a friend or a family member. The Indian woman's back is turned to me, to the photographer. No matter how good the intentions of the photographer were, no matter how good my own intentions are, one of the meanings of the photograph is genocide.

"I was in the airport," I stumbled. "I was on my way home from meeting Leona. She had told me about Indian ancestors."

"And that's what bothers me even more than the postcard," my other daughter said. "I just can't understand why you are so excited about having an Indian ancestor. You are a *white* woman."

"I'm not *'so excited . . .'*" I tried to say, at that moment not knowing what I was, but knowing that 'so excited' certainly wasn't right. "And of course I'm a white woman."

"Well, why aren't you going in search of your father's *Dutch* ancestors?"

My pain level was getting pretty high. This had been a lovely evening.

Now that my daughters and my son live at a distance in their own homes, it is a rare privilege to be with them. But something more than an evening of pizza and laughter and good talk was at stake here. I felt myself losing control. I cry when I am hurt, and I didn't want to cry in Bertucci's. We were finished eating; someone had eaten the last slice of pizza when I said, "I'm sorry, but I have to go. I want to walk home. The three of you can bring the car; I need to walk. I'll be fine — I just need to get my breath."

As I got up to leave, they said, "It's just a problem. The situation of Native Americans now is ignored . . ."

"And meanwhile they are exploited by those nostalgic photographs and by white people trying to claim Indian ancestors."

"We know that's not what you're doing, but its a *problem*."

Outside, it was mercifully cool and mercifully dark. As I crossed the little park that lies between Bertucci's and our house, I could let tears come, and they came with sobs so deep I felt like a child, bereft. Peter caught up with me, and walked beside me, keeping silence, for which I was grateful. The sobs seemed to come from very long ago, to connect me to a very old grief.

What was I searching for, anyway? What took me to Ireland, and to Missouri? A search for God, certainly. But what else? Grasshoppers, lightning bugs, oak trees. The vanished tabernacle. The everlasting creek. The Ozarks. At that moment, I was nothing but feelings, and the feelings were inarticulate. Later, I would talk again and again with my daughters and my son. I would talk with Enid Santiago Welch, my spiritual daughter, who has struggled with these questions. I would seek out Eunice Larrabee, a Lakota elder and national advocate for Native American rights, and ask her to tell me if my own search was inappropriate. Her gentle acceptance would come to me as a great gift.

In the privacy of my own soul, in the center of my own nights, I would ask what does it mean to be white? What does it mean to have

Wake Up Laughing

rivers of blood from many nations flowing in the inner geography of my dreams? Who am I? Does my whiteness make me a blank? I would learn that there are laws that decree that "white" is not a race. Whiteness is the invisible eye behind the camera, arranging the scene, interpreting it, naming it. Taking for itself the power of God. This is not something I personally did, but it is the culture I inherit. It is the position I cannot escape.

Is whiteness a blank? Am I a blank? Am I nothing? Am I just a crazy jigsaw puzzle of cultures that no one can piece together? Later, I would say that the songs of no single people can I claim as my people's songs. Each strand of my culture is a minor strand.

Later I would acknowledge that I have turned and looked at the face of my English forefather. I have seen his specific and actual power to kill peasants in Ireland, turn them out of their homes, starve them to death. But I am not him. Neither am I the immigrant Dutch ancestor who never learned to speak English. Her disorientation in a new land is not mine. Neither am I the ancestor with the Spanish name who owned slaves and commanded a company of rangers against Indians in Virginia. Neither am I the Native American ancestor whose culture was erased by the Dutch and English and Spanish and God only knows how many other ancestors of mine who engulfed this continent and named it after an Italian navigator. I am not any of those whose native names were erased from my country's history and from my family's history. I am not Native American.

Or am I all of these? Is the essence of who I am actually the mixed water of many tributaries, the river of my life muddy water, mixed water, but living, by God, *living* water.

Later, I would open my hands and my heart and admit that I do not know what it is to be white, but whatever it is, it is what I am. It is not nothing. It is not a blank. If I were floating by myself in outer space, I would have no race. I would be human, as opposed to planet, or star. But on this earth in this time I am an inheritor of race, and my race is white. My race is tainted by the actions of those who used it for power, created the divided city in which I was a child, the divided country in which my grandchildren live. Later I would come to believe that it is necessary for each one of us to listen to the tiniest tributaries of the rivers of blood, where they come from, in order to understand who we are and where we are going. All of the tributaries have their origins in the same mists of our beginnings. We come from dream and go to dream.

But those thoughts would be later. That night, walking toward home, Peter and I reached our street. Without speaking we moved under street lamps through pools of light and through larger pools of shadow. Gradually sobs gave way to words. "I have not been looking for an Indian," I said to him. "I have been looking for my grandmother. This is not about Native Americans. It's about my grandmother. They don't mean to, but they're doing the same thing my mother did. They're saying, *'You can't have her.'*"

37

I AM first and last a child of the crawdad, a child of the curled prehistoric fossil snail. Those ancestors, too, I visited in the creek of my childhood. Holiness there was intact. I have confirmed in my heart the sacredness of the rocks, the hills, the streams, the land that was my own first home.

That the form of the fossil snail I cherished in my childhood in the Ozarks is reflected in the curled triple spiral carved into rock by prehistoric human hands in Ireland, widens my sense of belonging to all people, and to all of the earth. Carl Jung said that human development is like a spiral. We come back again and again to the same place, but on a different level.

It has been good to turn and look back at the trail I myself walked with my own flesh-and-bone feet on my own ground. It has been good to see where my own footsteps begin, there where the footsteps of those before me are fading into the leaf mold.

It has been good, too, to listen to the wisdom of my children. Their generation has learned from my generation. I can take them to the past. They take me to the future.

For my birthday, two years after my visit to Missouri, my daughter Laurel gave me the gift of going with me one more time to see Leona before she died. We went first to Ava and visited the cemetery where my mother's people are buried. After we stood beside their graves and I introduced her to Aunt Nellie, Uncle Elmer, and my grandmother Emma Ridgway, we looked for the tombstone of "Cloud" Lakey. He was nowhere to be found. We walked up and down the paths between stones, Laurel searching one side and I searching the other. We got in the car and did the whole thing over again. I became more and more embarrassed and agitated. "I *know* he's here somewhere!" I cried. "I didn't just make the whole thing up!"

But increasingly, as we searched, I began to feel that perhaps, after all, the whole thing was a phantom, a ghost of my own making. Laurel comforted me. "Mom, it's OK. It's here somewhere. We just can't find it."

Then, having given up, and preparing to exit the cemetery, I saw a faint, two-track road between rows of stones near the gate, and instinctively I turned down it, as I must have turned on my first visit. At the end of the road, just before turning toward a second gate and leaving the cemetery grounds, there was a Lakey tombstone. But the name on it was not "Cloud." It was "Shade." And the laughter, this time, was not from the ghost of a corn-growing Indian. It was a grin, exchanged between a very flesh and blood mother and daughter, standing in the sun of a Missouri mid-day.

I like "Shade" better than "Cloud." In those rocky fields, in that intense summer heat, shade is precious. Cattle gather under oak trees, children play under bushes. Shade is a gentle word, and a "shade," after all, is a ghost.

W E went next to the cemetery at Waynesville, and stood beside the grave of Laurel's grandfather, my father. This time it was as it should be; I was the bridge between my father and my daughter. We were in our rightful places; I felt it as I stood beside his grave and spoke to her of "my father."

Wake Up Laughing

We found the churchyard where Elzina and Harv are buried, the tiny, handmade gravestones, the rocky earth. Finally we went unannounced to Leona's gravel road, drove slowly and in silence until we came to her trailer. No one was there. There was no bark from Pup to greet us; the place felt abandoned.

The porch was exactly as it had been, but across the two-by-four that acted as a rail was thrown a very old, faded quilt. I opened it out, hung it straight to see the pattern. The soft design of colors was complicated by another pattern superimposed on it by the sun and the trees around the trailer. Shadows of leaves fell across the cotton print pieces sewn together and faded to pastels. I lay my hand on it, bent to see the intricate rows of hand stitching, and wondered if it was the hand of my lost grandmother that had pushed the needle through scraps cut from house dresses and aprons.

We found Leona on a hospital bed, dying of emphysema and cancer. Bernice was beside her, and this time there was genuine warmth between my cousin and myself. Leona's dying cut through the distance between her daughter and me. I brought my daughter, and they received her as the gift that I intended her to be.

I could see in Bernice's face the bone structure, the coloring, the shape of my own. I no longer resisted her words, *"Sure is too bad you missed so much."* I simply felt grateful that she received me warmly into the moment that I was not missing.

What mattered now was Leona, and behind her my father and his mother and father, all slipping away again. What mattered, too, were the stories, the images that Leona would take with her. How few we had captured! How precious they were!

She was weak, but she seemed to want, as we did, the passing on of tradition. Bernice stood on one side of her bed, Laurel and I on the other. After a while our talk turned to the Native American ancestors, and Laurel asked Bernice if they were Cherokee.

"Yes," Bernice said. "Cherokee. That's what I was always told."

"I don't know," Leona said.

Some months before, while waiting for a bus one day in San Francisco, I had browsed in a bookstore and happened upon a book titled *The Trail of Tears*. Inside the front cover was a map of the brutal journey the Cherokees were forced to make from Tennessee to Oklahoma. It went through Missouri. It went very close to Ava. It went exactly through Waynesville.

Laurel and I had driven to Missouri from her home in Nashville, choosing the highway that allowed us to follow the Trail of Tears. We crossed the Mississippi River where the Trail had crossed it. There is a small museum there, and I asked a guide, "Did Cherokee people drop off of the march as it went through this area?"

"Oh, yes," she said. "People slipped away from the march at every opportunity. Cherokees settled all along the Trail."

The census for Douglas County, where I was born, showed more than six thousand Indians in 1934, the year of my birth. Only a few years later, there were almost none. What happened?

I believe shame happened. Leona's voice was scarcely more than a whisper. Laurel and I bent close to hear her say, "Them Lakey boys was bad. Real bad."

"What did they do?" Laurel asked.

"Oh, everything," Leona said.

We were anxious not to tire her, but a treasure was slipping away with her every breath. Laurel bent close, asked gently, "Can you tell us what they did?"

"Everything," Leona sighed. "Stealing, murder. They killed one whole family, children and all." She paused, thinking, and then said, "I guess it was the Indian in them."

Laurel and I looked at one another over her bed. There it was. What is believed by those in power finally filters down to those who are

Wake Up Laughing

powerless. *They say we are without worth; it must be true. I guess it was the Indian in them.*

As I was leaving, Leona took my hand and said, "Patsy, your Daddy loved you. A whole lot."

That night, driving back to the motel, we stopped seven times to rescue little box turtles from the highway. I had forgotten how many there are in the springtime in Missouri. My friend, Cindy Davenport, Alabama Muscogee, had shown us a video just before we left on our journey of a Muscogee (Creek) woman who makes the leg rattles worn for dancing. She uses old cowboy boots for the leggings, cutting away the feet and lacing the tops with leather cords. Each legging holds three box turtle shells full of gravel, so the dancer, pounding her feet in the dance, makes the most amazing racket. The woman says in the video that she finds the turtles on the road. She carries a bucket every day when she walks to the post office, and brings it home full of turtles.

Laurel and I were driving out of that country just as dusk darkened into night. We came to a field that was outlined at its far edges with oak trees, and she pulled over to the edge of the road, shut off the motor and rolled down the window. We sat listening to the throb of countless tree frogs and crickets, watching a million lightning bugs flickering above the field. Around us, the gentle hills of the Ozarks held us as if in the palm of a hand.

Laurel whispered, "I had no idea it was so beautiful."